BY THE SAME AUTHOR

(with Vanda Foster) Crinolines and Crimping Irons: Victorian Clothes –
How They Were Cleaned and Cared For

The Ghost in the Looking Glass: The Victorian Seamstress

The Way to Wear'em: 150 Years of *Punch* on Fashion

WELCOME SWEET BABE

A Book of Christenings

Christina Walkley

PETER OWEN · LONDON

ISBN 0 7206 0685 3

PETER OWEN PUBLISHERS
73 Kenway Road London SW5 0RE

First published 1987
© Christina Walkley 1987

Photoset and printed in Great Britain by
WBC Print Ltd Bristol

For Olivia

CONTENTS

ACKNOWLEDGEMENTS

Permission to use quoted material in this book has been granted by courtesy of the following:

W.H. Allen & Co. plc for extracts from *The Silver Road* by Mary Hamilton (originally published by Allan Wingate);

Cambridge University Press for extracts from *Fenland Chronicle* by Sybil Marshall;

David & Charles Publishers plc for an extract from *Crafts, Customs and Legends of Wales* by Mary Corbett Harris;

André Deutsch Ltd for an extract from *My Life's History* by Grandma Moses;

Farmers Weekly for recipes from *Farmhouse Fare*;

Michael Joseph Ltd for extracts from *Village Diary* by Miss Read;

Macmillan Inc., New York, for extracts from *O Rugged Land of Gold* by Martha Martin;

Oxford University Press for extracts from *Lark Rise to Candleford* by Flora Thompson and *Still Glides the Stream* by Flora Thompson;

Alan Sutton Publishing Ltd for extracts from *Paupers and Pig Killers: The Diary of William Holland a Somerset Parson 1799–1818*, edited by Jack Ayres.

The illustrations listed below (identified by page references) are reproduced by kind permission, as noted: p. 26, Society of Antiquaries, London: p. 29, City Art Gallery, Manchester; p. 80, Tate Gallery, London; p. 81, Collection at Parham Park, West Sussex; pp. 73, 84 and 87, Gallery of English Costume, Manchester City Art Galleries; pp. 126 and 128, by gracious permission of Her Majesty the Queen.

If you live as I do in the country, a long way away from comprehensive libraries, you are faced as a researcher with various practical problems. I am deeply grateful to the people who have offered solutions to some of these, whether by hunting out material, lending me books, offering me hospitality or looking after my children: Jane Badger, Penelope Byrde, Beryl and Ken Cholmondeley, Catherine, Felicity and Matthew Eden, Russell Edwards, Peter Farrer, Sue Fudge, Pearl Hackett, Jocelyn and Peter Hallinan, Angela Hamm, Colin Hardie, Elizabeth, Frederic, Genevieve and Oliver Hawkins, Di Hooley, Anthea Jarvis, Frances Moule, Mr and Mrs Nelson, Gerald Pitman, Cynthia Sartin, Robbie Stok, Julian Treuherz, Derek Valentine, Isobel Walker, Harold and Nancy Walkley, Carolyn Waterfall, Caroline and Charles Worth, and the staff of Bristol Central and Storrington Libraries.

I am especially indebted to Steven Ferdinando for letting me use his bookshop like a lending library, to Diana Hawkins for her help with the pattern for the christening robe in Appendix 2, and to the Revd Peter Hooper for advice on matters of doctrine.

Most of all I want to thank Phill, George and Henry who, each in their different ways, gave me their loving support, and Toby who, by arranging to be born and christened while this book was in progress, turned it into a personal and wholly delightful project.

C.W.

INTRODUCTION

Array'd - a half-angelic sight
In vests of pure baptismal white,
The mother to the font doth bring
The little helpless, nameless thing
With hushes soft and mild caressing,
At once to get - a name and blessing.

Charles Lamb, *The Christening*

The word christening immediately conjures up a picture of a baby in a long white robe, of silver spoons and cups, and perhaps of a white-iced cake with pale blue or pink decorations. But what exactly is a christening? Essentially it is an occasion on which the sacrament of baptism is administered to a baby, thus effecting its formal introduction into the Christian Church. Because the baby is too young to speak for itself, it is represented at the ceremony by sponsors or godparents who make the responses and assume the responsibilities on its behalf. The service includes a naming ritual. Today children are registered at birth and christened, for the most part, when they are a few months old. Yet while in the past the ceremony was the occasion when the name was first made known, and was therefore of great importance, it has now lost much of its significance.

The baptizing of babies has a tradition nearly as old as Christianity itself, and over the years the religious celebration became encrusted with extraneous customs and beliefs. Some were actually pagan, and stemmed from the sometimes uneasy grafting of Christianity on to older beliefs; others were merely secular, offshoots of the festivities attending a new birth. For, as well as being a Church ceremony, a christening soon

11

came to be seen as a joyful social occasion on which a birth could be celebrated.

Primarily, then, a christening is a religious event. Baptism traces its origins directly back to John's baptizing of Jesus in the River Jordan, and most Christians recognize it as a sacrament – that is, as an 'outward and visible sign of inward and spiritual grace', the two notable exceptions being the Society of Friends and the Salvation Army, which reject the whole concept of sacraments. Baptism itself is almost universal, yet its administration varies widely from Church to Church. Water is an essential component of the ritual, but while in some communities the candidate will be merely sprinkled with it, in others he will be totally immersed. And the age of the candidate is also variable, since not all Churches hold with infant baptism. George Eliot's Silas Marner, from a 'narrow religious sect', when urged by Dolly Winthrop to get his foundling baby christened,

> . . . was puzzled and anxious, for Dolly's word 'christened' conveyed no distinct meaning to him. He had only heard of baptism, and had only seen the baptism of grown-up men and women.
>
> 'What is it as you mean by "christened"?' he said at last timidly. 'Won't folks be good to her without it?'
>
> 'Dear, dear, Master Marner!' said Dolly, with gentle distress and compassion. 'Had you never no father nor mother as taught you to say your prayers, and as there's good words and good things to keep us from harm?'
>
> 'Yes,' said Silas in a low voice; 'I know a deal about that – used to, used to. But your ways are different; my country was a good way off.' He paused a few moments, and then added more decidedly, 'But I want to do everything as can be done for the child; and whatever's right for it i' this country, and you think 'ull do it good, I'll act according, if you'll tell me.'
>
> 'Well, then, Master Marner,' said Dolly, inwardly rejoiced, 'I'll ask Mr. Macey to speak to the parson about it; and you must fix on a name for it, because it must have a name giv' it when it's christened.'

In the United States there has always been a similar variety of practice. This is vividly illustrated in the recollections of Grandma Moses:

> There was a little Episcopal chapel near the Dangerfield place [in Virginia], we used to go across the meadow to the chapel. . . . All denominations would come there on communion day, Presbyterians, Baptists, Methodists, and Unitarian brothers, all took communion, there was no partiality one way or the other. . . . That's where we were all baptized. Thomas [her husband] had been baptized, but the rest of us hadn't. I did it because I thought it wasn't right not to be all one. We stood by the altar, and the minister just sprinkled us. It didn't make any difference with me, didn't change me. It wasn't customary to baptize children, I don't remember ever hearing of anyone being baptized until I was well grown up, only certain people were. Way back in my grandmother's day [the early nineteenth century] they must have had baptism, because I heard of her telling me of the dresses the children wore over in the Cambridge church. And up here the Baptists wait till they are big enough to dip them under water six feet down. There was a good many baptized here several years ago right out in the Owl Kill, the minister would dip them in over their heads and say a prayer, and then they'd heel it home to get on dry clothes.

In England, owing to the existence of an established Church, people have always tended to consider themselves as Church of England unless proved otherwise. Thus at the end of the nineteenth century Flora Thompson observed that 'if the Lark Rise people had been asked their religion, the answer of nine out of ten would have been "Church of England", for practically all of them were christened, married, and buried as such, although, in adult life, few went to church between the baptisms of their offspring'. In this climate religious practice frequently became a matter of social convention rather than of deeply felt belief. It was exactly the same story in Catholic France. Some of the clergy were infuriated by the complacent claiming of the Church's amenities without any of its discipline. The parish priest in Zola's *La Terre*, goaded beyond endurance by his utterly indifferent and amoral flock, explodes at the Buteau christening party: 'Well! I've threatened you often enough, this time I'm leaving, and I shan't come back. . . . We shall see who'll lose out. You can live without a priest, like animals. . . . I know for sure that your cattle are more religious than you are. . . . Goodbye! and you can baptize your heathen brat by sousing it in the pond!' In the end he is persuaded to perform the ceremony, the mother protesting that 'only dogs don't get baptized', but he rushes through it at breakneck speed and leaves the family breathless.

It was not only the laity who could become disaffected. In the seventeenth century the Manx islanders complained that 'the sick are not visited; parties dying without prayers, exhortations and the Holy Communion, though much desired by the sick. Children weak and strong have to be taken to other parishes for their christendom and to pay for it'. And in Hardy's *Under the Greenwood Tree* the villagers lament the passing of the old parson with his lax ways and express their resentment of his conscientious successor:

'And he was a very honourable man in not wanting any of us to come and hear him if we were all on-end for a jaunt or spree, or to bring the babies to be christened if they were inclined to squalling. There's good in a man's not putting a parish to unnecessary trouble.'

'And there's this here man never letting us have a bit o' peace; but keeping on about being good and upright till 'tis carried to such a pitch as I never see the like of afore nor since!'

'No sooner had he got here than he found the font wouldn't hold water, as it hadn't for years off and on; and when I told him that Mr. Grinham never minded it, but used to spet upon his vinger and christen 'em just as well, 'a said, "Good Heavens! Send for a workman immediate. What place have I come to!" Which was no compliment to us, come to that.'

In the past parents had their children christened as a matter of course unless they belonged to a sect that disallowed infant baptism, and even then they might find themselves bullied into conformity by their local parson. William Holland noted triumphantly in his diary for 1807: 'Mrs Hurley brought another child to Church to be Baptized and she herself was Churched. They have a vast number of children and are Anabaptists and I made them bring four or five to be Christened at one time and they continue to bring them to Church but go generally to the Meeting House. However it is gaining something to be Baptized at our Church.' Today the clergy have no such power, and social pressures are unlikely to propel indifferent people into insincere churchgoing, yet even in these secularized times one in three babies born in Britain still gets baptized. Obviously many of these children come from non-Christian families, and this poses a problem for the officiating priest. The *Book of Common Prayer* (1662) ordains that 'no Minister shall refuse or . . . delay to baptize any infant within his cure that is brought to the church to be baptized', but if it is clear that the professions and undertakings are neither sincerely made nor will be faithfully fulfilled, the service has no meaning. Faced with this dilemma, some of the clergy are demanding a drastic rethinking of the whole issue. In a letter to the *Church Times* (January 1987), the founder of the 'Movement for the Reform of Infant Baptism' made an impassioned plea against the indiscriminate christening of babies and urged that adult baptism should become the norm. Change in matters of religious practice is notoriously slow to achieve, and in the interim many priests are achieving a compromise solution: they do not withhold a religious ceremony from anyone who asks for one, but they use, instead of the actual baptism, the service of thanksgiving for the birth of a child which is provided in *The Alternative Service Book* of 1980.

What are parents looking for when they ask for their child to be christened? Those who are practising Christians are probably pretty clear about it, and for many more, whose religion is residual, and who would be hard put to it to define the doctrine involved, it is a way of expressing their gratitude for the gift of a child. But a great many people simply feel that the birth of a child is too special and important an event to go unmarked, and they turn to the Church because it alone caters for their need. There is as yet no secular counterpart to the christening, the registration of the child's birth and name being a brief and unemotional formality. An interesting attempt to provide an alternative ceremony was made at the end of the nineteenth century. John Trevor, a one-time Unitarian minister from Manchester, founded the so-called 'Labour Churches' in 1891, with a view to fulfilling the traditional role of the Church within a political, not a religious, context. Recognizing the vital importance of rites of passage as a means of creating fellowship and group identity, Trevor provided for these in his organization. A christening (the traditional word was used) was held in Leeds in 1895: 'Our president officiated, who, in a little impressive speech, gave the child its name (Alice), hoping that when it grew so as to be able to take its place in the Battle of Life, she would be found in the ranks of the "despised", if they be fighting for Love, Truth and Justice.'

Thus a christening, as well as being a religious event, is essentially a social one. Right up until the twentieth century it was the baby's first public appearance. Birth is private. Custom dictates who shall be there to support the mother, whether it be her husband, her own mother, the other women of her community, a doctor, or in the case of poor Queen Victoria a whole roomful of people including the Prime Minister and the Archbishop of Canterbury; but it is never open house. Birth is too unpredictable a process for that, and even when it has reached a happy conclusion the mother is generally too exhausted to want to celebrate immediately with family and friends. A christening is the public face of childbirth, and an assertion that the baby has been born not just into a particular family but into the whole community. This is the point behind the Church's general insistence on administering baptism during one of the regular Sunday services, and having the whole congregation join in the responses and welcome the child into their midst. Christenings are for sharing. Martha Martin, completely alone with her baby in the wilds of an Alaskan winter, nevertheless held a proper christening party for her (as we shall see later), complete with a white robe, a present, and a feast, which was shared by the local wildlife.

Ironically, because it was once considered imperative to baptize babies as soon as they were born, mothers were for a long time excluded from the celebrations because they were still too weak to participate. Well-meaning attempts in the seventeenth and eighteenth centuries to include the mother by holding the christening party in her bedroom often backfired because, as a French obstetrician of the time commented, 'though there is scarce any of the company, which do not drink her health, yet by the noise they make in her ears, she loses it'. It was not until Victorian times that christening was deferred until the baby was a few weeks old, and the party changed from being a more or less alcoholic gathering of the father and his cronies to an afternoon tea for all the family. Large families were not, of course, a Victorian innovation, but the Victorians responded to them in a new way, following the example of their Queen with her deep commitment to domesticity. Children were not dragged so hurriedly into adulthood as before, and an autonomous nursery culture sprang up. The home became the object of an almost religious cult, with family occasions like birthdays and christenings as its festivals.

Christenings could not be performed publicly in church where the child's health was at risk, but home baptisms were supposed to be for cases of emergency only. In 1810 Parson Holland noted in his diary:

> Porter's wife in the Poorhouse is brought to bed this morning and in a short time afterwards the woman who nurses it brought the child to me to have a name, as they term it in these parts. I answered if the child was ill I was ready to give it a Private Baptism but not otherwise for we were forbidden to do so except in cases of necessity. She thought it was not well, did not eat. Let me see the child. A finer child I never saw. If I was to Christen it before it is brought to Church every parent in the Parish would expect the same and Publick Baptism in the Church would come to Nothing. So she was dismissed and I hear no more of the child.

Even when a private baptism had been allowed, the child was supposed to be brought to church at a later date for it to be ratified. In 1777 Parson Woodforde complained: 'Harry Dunnell behaved very impertinent this morning to me because I would not privately name his child for him, he having one child before named privately by me and never had it brought to Church afterwards. He had the Impudence to tell me that he would send it to some Meeting House to be named etc. – very saucy indeed.'

Christenings, then, are religious occasions, and they are also public and social occasions. However, it would be a pity to close the subject without mentioning the obvious fact that they are essentially joyful occasions too. There are of course exceptions; for example, the pathetic Welsh 'coffin christenings', recorded as late as 1934, where if a mother had died in childbirth her baby was baptized in a bowl of water on top of the coffin; or the Hanoverian royal christenings, which triggered off dramatic family quarrels. And both Thomas Hardy in a poem, and

D.H. Lawrence in a short story, used a christening as a focus for social and domestic tension. But exceptions they are. The vast majority of christenings, as will be apparent from the pages that follow, are times of happiness and celebration, when the parents share with family and friends their jubilation and gratitude 'for the wonder and joy of creation . . . for the life of [their] child, for a safe delivery, and for the privilege of parenthood'.

1

THE CEREMONY

Grant to this child the inward grace,
While we the outward sign impart;
The Cross we on his forehead trace
Do Thou engrave upon his heart.

May it his pride and glory be,
Beneath Thy banner fair unfurl'd,
To march to certain victory
O'er sin, o'er Satan, o'er the world.

Hymns Ancient and Modern

From the earliest days of Christianity baptism was the rite whereby new converts, after a long and rigorous training, were admitted to full membership of the Christian community. After a fast and vigil, the candidate made a confession of his sins and renounced the Devil, following which he was immersed in water to symbolize the washing away of his guilt, baptized in the name of the Trinity, and then given a white robe to put on that represented the new and sinless life into which he had been reborn.

The first converts to Christianity were of course adults, and so there is no mention in the earliest records of babies being baptized. It is on these grounds that some Christian groups, including the Anabaptists of the sixteenth century, the Mennonites, the Disciples of Christ and present-day Baptists, have rejected infant baptism, holding that it can have no value or meaning where the recipient is too young to understand or participate. A further objection was the belief, voiced by the Christian writer Tertullian early in the third century AD, that it was wellnigh impossible to gain forgiveness for sins committed after baptism. The sacrament was therefore deferred as long as possible, sometimes until the point of death. St Augustine is a case in point. His mother, St Monica, brought him up on Christian principles but did not have him baptized, 'in the surmise that, if I continued to live, I should defile myself again with sin and, after baptism, the guilt of pollution would be greater and more dangerous'. As a child he became gravely ill with a stomach disorder and begged his mother for baptism, but when she was on the point of yielding he recovered, and so it was put off again. In later life Augustine was critical of this decision:

> Why do we continually hear people say, even nowadays, 'Leave him alone and let him do it. He is not yet baptized'? Yet when the health of the body is at stake, no one says 'Let him get worse. He is not yet cured.' It would, then, have been much better if I had been healed at once and if all that I and my family could do had been done to make sure that once my soul had received its salvation, its safety should be left in your keeping, since its salvation had come from you.

Whatever the disagreements between theologians may have been, the majority of Christian communities adopted infant baptism from an early date – the third-century scholar Origen mentions it as an established practice in his day. If the baby was going to be baptized, the very high rate of perinatal mortality made it imperative for it to be done at once. Medieval babies were nearly always christened on the day they were born. If their health allowed, they were carried to church by the midwife, accompanied by the godparents, friends and neighbours who had been hastily convened. Once arrived at the church, the midwife undressed the baby on a cushioned table – in cold weather there might be a fire to do this by – and handed him to the godfather, who held him while the priest signed him on the forehead with holy oil and recited the words of the service, after which the priest plunged him into the water of the font. The midwife then took him back, hushed his cries, dried and dressed him, after which he was taken back home to his mother, who was of course still lying in while this was going on. But if the baby was weak and ailing, a trip to church would be too hazardous. The priest might be summoned to the house, but in case he could not arrive in time there were emergency procedures to be followed. Edmund of Abingdon,

Baptism, from a late fourteenth-century manuscript

Archbishop of Canterbury from 1233, laid down that when childbirth became imminent, the parents were to prepare a vessel and some water so that no time should be lost. In addition priests had a duty to instruct all layfolk how to administer the sacrament in the vernacular, and it was an archdeacon's job to check that this was done. In practice the task usually fell to the midwife, who thus carried a double responsibility for the child's physical and spiritual survival. The essential thing was that she should remember the exact words, without which the whole sacrament was invalidated. A terrible story was circulated of a midwife who, when baptizing a dying baby, in her panic had used the words 'St John' instead of 'Holy Trinity', and had thus debarred the child from Paradise.

There were exceptions to same-day baptism. On Holy Saturday and the Saturday before Whitsun all fonts were solemnly blessed, and babies who had been born in the previous week were supposed to wait to be baptized until after the blessing, provided they were not in danger of death. But there were also laws which suggest that, left to themselves, not all parents were as assiduous as they might have been in this matter.

Saxon law decreed that children must be baptized within thirty days of birth, on pain of a 30s. fine (a huge sum then), and if a child died unbaptized the father had to pay compensation of all he owned. The tenth-century *Canons of Edgar* allowed thirty-seven days, but this was subsequently shortened to a week. Even as late as 1624 William Green, a Catholic, had to pay a fine of £100 to an ecclesiastical court for failing to have his child baptized in the parish church within a month of its birth, though at this time the law was enforced less out of immediate concern for the child's salvation than as a means of undermining opposition to the established Church.

In earliest times baptism was by immersion, the font consisting of a large sunken basin in which the candidate stood while more water was poured over him. This basin often stood in a chapel separate from the main body of the church, called a baptistery. When infant baptism began to be common, the basin was raised off the ground to make it easier for the

St John baptizing a youth, from an English manuscript *c.* 1230.

priest to immerse the child. There once stood in the baptistery of the Cathedral of St John in Florence a font of a curious design, but this was destroyed in 1576. Apparently it was similar to one discovered at Pistoia in 1965, and consisted of a marble pedestal with a hole in each corner and one in the middle, each hole just under 3 feet deep and about 15 inches across. It has been suggested that in the course of the mass baptisms held, as noted above, on the vigil of Easter and Pentecost, the priests stood in the four corner fonts and immersed the children in the central one, thus keeping clear of the crowding congregation. Dante tells us that on one occasion a child got stuck in one of the fonts and would have drowned or suffocated had not Dante himself smashed the marble surround and released him (an action that later incurred malicious charges of sacrilege from his enemies).

From about the eighth century onwards the method of affusion became a possible alternative to immersion. This merely involved pouring a small quantity of water over the candidate's head. The adoption of this practice may well have been prompted by concern for the candidates' health, particularly if they were new-born babies. That this concern was well founded is illustrated by an incident in New England history. The Revd Charles Chauncy, one-time Fellow of Trinity College, Cambridge, who emigrated to North America in the 1640s, brought with him his strong views on the desirability of total immersion. To this the Fathers of the colony replied firmly that the climate was too harsh. A dispute ensued, which came to a head at the christening of Governor Winthrop's twins. Chauncy insisted on immersing the babies, as a result of which one of them lost consciousness, moving Winthrop to very understandable fury. Eventually, after a great deal more disagreement and bad feeling, Chauncy was offered the presidency of Harvard on condition that he kept his views on baptism to himself. The bribe proved irresistible, and immersion was dropped.

The *Book of Common Prayer* makes specific provision for fragile babies, ruling that 'if [the godparents] shall certify [the priest] that the Child may well endure it he shall dip it in the Water discreetly and warily. . . . But if they certify that the Child is weak, it shall suffice to pour Water upon it'. This resulted in a change in font design. Instead of the large basin in which a man could stand, all that was needed now was a free-standing bowl over which the priest could hold the child high enough to make the pouring of the water easy. But even when a small quantity of water was used, the procedure could still be thoroughly uncomfortable for the baby. In Flora Thompson's *Still Glides the Stream* Mrs Truman tips the clerk a shilling to warm the water for little Polly's christening, and at Paul Dombey's, 'the clerk (the only cheerful-looking object there, and *he* was an undertaker) came up with a jug of warm water, and said something, as he poured it into the font, about taking the chill off; which millions of gallons boiling hot could not have done for the occasion'. Where these precautions were not taken, the parson might well find, as Kilvert did on St Valentine's Eve, 1870, that the font was full of floating chunks of ice.

Where baptisms were performed privately, a substitute for the font had to be found. Bishop Quevil ruled in 1287 that when a baby had had to be baptized at home, the vessel that had been used to hold the water should either be given to the Church or destroyed by fire. This suggests that such vessels were credited with magic properties and that the Bishop was afraid they would be used for sinister purposes. But later, christening cups were often treasured for many generations precisely because they had been used as part of the rite of baptism. The most surprising substitute for a font appeared at Carola Oman's christening in 1897. She was the first child to be baptized in the chapel of All Souls College, but as the Fellows had always been celibate, there was no font. She was therefore christened in the College's largest punch-bowl.

The Reformation did not substantially alter the service of baptism, with the exception of the anointing with oil, which was left out. Otherwise the essentials were the same, though the details were different; but this was sufficient to provoke deep suspicion on both sides about each other's ceremonies. The diarist John Evelyn attended the christening of Sir Samuel Tuke's son Charles which, he remarked disparagingly, 'was don at Somerset House by a *Popish Priest* with many odd Ceremonies, Spittle and anointings'. 'Spittle' is a reference to a curious tradition whereby the priest spat in the child's mouth. When Mary Queen of Scots' son James was baptized the Queen 'did inhibit' this practice, saying, it was later reported, that she would not have a 'pocky priest' spitting in her child's mouth. Differences in religious practice could also fuel matrimonial disputes. Pepys recorded in 1662 that

. . . Mrs. Sarah told me how the falling out between my Lady Castlemaine and her Lord was about christening the child lately [afterwards called Charles Fitzroy], which he would have, and had done by a [Catholic] priest: and, some days after, she had it again christened by a minister; the King, and Lord of Oxford, and Duchesse of Suffolk, being witnesses; and christened with a proviso, that it had not already been christened. Since that she left her Lord, carrying away every thing in the house; so much as every dish, and cloth, and servant but the porter. He is gone discontented into France, they say, to enter a monastery; and now she is coming back again to her house in King-street.

During the Commonwealth drastic changes in religious practice were enforced. The use of *The Book of Common Prayer* was forbidden under pain of fine or imprisonment, only secular marriages were allowed, and in the parish registers children were entered under their date of birth, not of baptism. The Puritans rejected the idea of godparents and the use of the sign of the cross, and although from 1645 the registers refer to 'pouring or sprinckling of water' in church, this was not to be done in 'the places where Fonts in the time of Popery were unfitly and superstitiously placed'. Those who adhered to the old ways opted for a private service which would attract as little attention as possible: John Evelyn's children were baptized at home at Says Court, the first in the 'little drawing roome, next the Parlor', the second in the library, the fourth in the 'withdrawing-roome'. In the first three cases the ceremony was performed by a Mr Owen, the 'sequestered' (i.e. dispossessed) Parson of Eltham. But it was an anxious time, and parents wondered what to do for the best. In 1647 Sir Ralph Verney wrote from France to his pregnant wife Mary:

Have a parson ready to christen the childe (any way will satisfye mee soe it bee christened) the best way to prevent all dainger & avoyde all trouble, will bee to dispatch it [i.e. the christening] as soone as it is borne, & that as privately as may bee. . . . I know not whither godfathers & godmothers are used now in England; tis noe great matter if they are not, but if they bee take Harry, Dr. or any other that are next at hand. . . . Bee sure the childe's name bee entred in ye

the generall assembly, and church of the first borne, which are written in heauen: and to God the iudge of all; and to the spirits of iust men made perfect. 24. And to Iesus the mediatour of the new couenant; and to the blood of sprinckling that spea : keth better things then that of Abel.

A christening in 1624. The baby is wrapped in a lace-edged bearing cloth.

Church booke to prevent all questions heerafter.

Mary replied: 'And for the suddaine crisning I will obay thee, and gett a minester in the house that will doe itt in the old way, for tis nott the fashion heare to have godfathers or godmothers, butt for the father to bring the child to church and answer for itt.'

But Ralph was nervous:

Now for the Christening. I pray give noe offence to the State; should it be donn in the old way perhapps it may bring more trouble uppon you then you can immagen, and all to noe purpose, for soe it bee donn with common ordinarie water, and that these words, 'I baptise thee in the name of the Father, and of the Sonne, and of the Holy Ghost', bee used with the water, I know the child is well baptised.

And he added philosophically: 'All the rest is but matter of forme and cerimoney which differs almost in every country, and though I must needs like one forme better then another, yet wee must not bee soe wedded to any thing of that nature, as to breake the union by a needlesse seperation in such indifferent things of the Church.'

Since a major element of the baptismal ceremony is the welcoming of the child into the Christian community, the Church has always urged that it should take place in a church, as part of one of the regular services, and in front of the congregation, unless there are pressing reasons against it. Many churches, especially in the last century, set aside particular Sundays and baptized numbers of children together. In Charlotte M. Yonge's novel *The Daisy Chain*, 'the usual Stoneborough fashion was to collect all the christenings for the month into one Sunday, except those for such persons as thought themselves too refined to see their children christened before the congregation, and who preferred an empty church and a weekday'. In the City Art Gallery, Manchester, there is a charming painting by James Charles, entitled *Christening Sunday*, which shows two christening parties coming out of a country church. But parents with social pretensions wanted something a little more special, and many of them insisted on a home christening. Thus in well-to-do homes in the seventeenth and eighteenth centuries the mother's bedroom was the traditional venue for a christening. This had the ostensible advantage that she herself was able to be present, but in practice she may well have found that after the pain and exhaustion of her confinement the noise and excitement of a party were the last things she wanted. Pepys noted in 1667 that 'we went by water to Michell's, and there his little house full of his father and mother and the kindred, hardly any else, and mighty merry in this innocent company, and Betty mighty pretty in bed, but, her head akeing, not very merry, but the company mighty merry, and I with them, and so the child christened'. But many people disapproved of this emphasis on the social and secular aspects of the occasion. Pepys's contemporary Evelyn was slightly apologetic about having been christened at home: 'The sollemnity yet (upon what accident I know not, unless some indisposition in me) was perform'd in the Dining rome by Parson Higham the present incumbent of the Parish.' Yet his own eight children all had home baptisms, and only the four eldest were born during the Commonwealth. Since the younger ones were christened between four and ten days after birth, they cannot have been in delicate health, so it must have been simply a whim of their parents not to have them taken to church. Despite this, Evelyn was highly critical when others tried to follow his example. In 1689 he noted in his diary that during a conversation with the Bishop of St Asaph and the Archbishop of Canterbury he had suggested that

> . . . the Baptising in private Houses, without necessity, might be reformd . . . proceeding meerely from the pride of [the] Women, bringing that into Custome, which was onely indulged in case of iminent danger: & out of necessity, during the Rebellion and persecution of the Cleargy, in our late Civil Warres &c: . . . [and] the Avarice of the Minister[s], who . . . were paid with considerable advantage & gifts, for baptising in Chambers: To this the two Bishops, heartily assented: and promised their indeavours to get it reformed: utterly disliking both practice[s], as novel, & undecent.

A century and a half later Cecilia Ridley agonized over a home versus a church christening for her baby, before deciding that she must practise what she preached:

> Now for the christening. You know Matt wished to have it on our wedding day, and we thought old Mr. Burrell was so very infirm he would not be able to walk to the church. Besides which we had some slight fears as to Baby in that cold damp place. So, much against my conscience and my wish, we settled to have it in the house. However, on Sunday, Mr. Bastard preached against the practice of baptising in houses – very strongly too – so that we felt quite ashamed of ourselves. And then we found there was a difficulty about another person performing the ceremony in his parish, so we decided to have it on Thursday in the church. Mr. Burrell was only to come in the afternoon on Wednesday, and accordingly it took place there, and most heartily glad am I that we did so settle it, for I think it was much more satisfactory and right, both for our own sakes and as an example, particularly as the Archdeacon has been anxious to discourage the private baptism. Baby was very good indeed and only

Christening Sunday, 1887, by James Charles (1851–1906)

gave one little squeak. Mr. Burrell got to church very well and it was not cold and everyone was delighted it should be there instead of in the house.

After the Middle Ages baptism was administered on the day of birth only if the baby was in danger of death. Parson Woodforde records a sad instance in 1768:

> I went over to C. Cary this night after eleven o'clock and privately baptised a child born this day and very dangerously ill in convulsions, by name George, of Perry's a Mason and a poor man in South Cary. . . . Never did I any ecclesiastical duty with more pleasure as it gave such great satisfaction to its Parents, and that they were so good and charitably disposed to have it done. The poor innocent Babe was taken with a violent fit, immediately after I had named it, and I really thought was dead, but it pleased God to restore it again, which was undoubtedly a blessing from Heaven for their goodness.

But alas, the very next day he wrote: 'The poor little Infant which I privately baptized last night departed this world this afternoon'; and the day after that: 'After Cary Service I buried that little Infant which I privately named two days ago', adding, rather startlingly to modern ears, '2 days old, a very happy turn for the dear Innocent.'

But if the baby was reasonably healthy, baptism was deferred, and gradually the time-lag grew longer. The children of John Evelyn were all baptized between three and twelve days after birth, but when the baptism of one of his grandchildren was put off for a whole month owing to the illness of his daughter and the absence of one of the godfathers, he was far from happy about it. An episode in *Wedded Life*, an edifying serial run by *The Ladies' Treasury* in the 1860s, makes it clear that by this time even devout parents were prepared to wait longer still. The heroine's mother criticizes her for having let her baby son reach the age of six weeks 'without having seen him enrolled among the soldiers of the cross'. Geraldine throws the blame on to the godparents (all titled), who will not commit themselves to a date for the ceremony; but Mrs Vernon, clearly opining that simple faith is worth more than Norman blood, questions their suitability to be godparents at all, and then proceeds to terrify her daughter with the awful story of a couple who deferred their child's christening for worldly reasons:

> The Onslows had been married fifteen years, and had no child to inherit their fine property. At last a boy was born to them. One would have thought that in gratitude for so great and long-coveted a boon, they would at the earliest opportunity, have dedicated it to the Lord. Not so. There was a very rich old lady in the Highlands, distantly related to Colonel Onslow, who had no children. They thought if she were to be asked to be godmother to their child, she might feel an interest in it, and make it her heir. They invited her to come to Onslow Hall, and be one of the sponsors. She promised to do so, but put it off from time to time. Anxious to secure what they thought a great good to their child, the parents waited and waited. At last she wrote to say, that feeling too infirm for so long a journey, she invited the child, the parents, and all connected with the christening, to her castle in the North; and added that she intended (being related as she was to the colonel, and having no heir of her own) to leave her property and estates to her future godchild; and that as soon as he had received at the font the name she intended to give him, she would make her will in his favour. The parents – short-sighted and worldly – were in high glee at this announcement. The party set out for the North; but whether so long a journey was too exciting for so young a brain, or whether there was a predisposition to disease, I do not know, but the very night of the child's arrival at the castle, and the eve of the christening, it was seized with violent convulsions, and *died* before medical assistance could be obtained. It died, Geraldine; and died unbaptised. I do not wish to dwell on a subject so distressing and so suggestive; but as in the midst of life we are in death, and the child blooming in health to-day may be a corpse tomorrow, I wish you to consult Launcelot, and not to be guided by worldly interest and ambition in a matter that concerns the spiritual welfare of your precious infant.

Despite such grim warnings, most parents were in no rush to get their children christened. By the turn of the century, *Etiquette of Today* was suggesting between four and eight weeks as a suitable age for the ceremony, but stressed that there was no fixed rule. Today most Catholics still prefer to baptize their children while they are small babies, but in the Church of England the age range is limitless. The practice of group christenings in the late nineteenth and early twentieth century is an indication of the increasing laxity in this area. Sybil Marshall recalled, in her *Fenland Chronicle*, that

> . . . we had a cousin as were born the very morning of the old queen's jubilee, so she were called Jubilee Anne, and when she were christened, we were all christened with her. My father were a curious man, and had all sorts of queer ideas, specially if they could be opposite to other folks'es, and he wouldn't have us children christened. My mother used to worry about it, and somehow or other she got her own way, so we were done with Jubilee Anne.

She was then seven. In South Wales it seems to have been quite common to baptize all the children of one family together: on 10 August 1873 William Thomas, a steelworker at Penydarren, had seven children christened, and on 1 December 1881 George and Leah Morgan had five. In some cases a whole street joined together for the occasion. Thus on 20 January 1898 seven children were christened who belonged to four families, all living in Gibson Row, Penydarren. In these cases obviously only the youngest participants would be babies, while the eldest might be quite big children.

Infant baptism places a great responsibility on the godparents. It is they who speak for the child, promise on his behalf to renounce evil, and undertake to see to it that he receives a Christian upbringing. In Catholic France it is quite common for young children to stand godparent to their baby brother or sister, but this has never been the case in England. Parents can sponsor their own child, but one Victorian writer pointed out the fundamental unsuitability of such a practice:

> I remember a poor, ignorant woman, in a village in Somersetshire, arguing with an earnest young clergyman, who had right views of such matters, that as she had been godmother to her nine others, under the old rector, there was no reason why she should not be so, too, to her tenth. 'Who so natural, your reverence,' she said, with all

the obstinacy of ignorance, 'as the blessed babe's own mother, as was godmother to all the others?' 'And suppose you were to die,' said the young clergyman, 'who is to see to the religious training and teaching of your little ones?' 'I never thought of that,' she replied; 'I'll ask a good friend of mine, a regular churchgoer, and will do her duty by my child, in case of anything happening to me.' 'Whether you live or die,' said the young rector, 'it is the sponsor's duty to see to the spiritual teaching and training of the child for whom she is answerable at the font.'

Because of the solemn nature of the undertaking, *The Book of Common Prayer* stipulates that godparents should themselves have been baptized and confirmed, so that they may 'faithfully fulfil their responsibilities both by their care for the child . . . and by the example of their own godly living', but with a proviso that the requirement for confirmation may be waived at the minister's discretion. Parson Holland noted indignantly in his diary for 1812: 'I had a Christening after Prayers and to my great surprize Sally Pocock who had been a servant of mine and was objected to on account of never having been Baptised offered to stand. I said it could not be for how can you answer for another who have never been Baptized yourself. So Mrs Crook the grandmother of the child stood.' Today the matter is approached more pragmatically, but most clergymen will inquire into the beliefs of those proposing to be godparents, and will wish to be satisfied that they view their undertaking with sufficient seriousness.

Speaking of the choice of godparents, a Victorian commentator complained that 'it is a difficult thing to ask people. The modern idea that has encrusted the ecclesiastical idea is, that the godfather should present a silver mug, or knife, fork, or spoon, or something of that kind, and sponsorship becomes a serious tax on one's benevolence. . . . It would be much better if it were understood all round that nothing of the kind was either expected or desired'. But this was not a modern idea at all – godparents had always been expected to provide a handsome present. In the Middle Ages the Church had to restrict the number of godparents to three, precisely because of the general tendency to enlist every available wealthy acquaintance in order that the child should be well provided for. The Church of England continued this practice, specifying that each child should have two sponsors of its own, and one of the opposite, sex; while in the Catholic Church it is usual to have one of each. Royal babies are a conspicuous exception to this rule, and generally have lots of sponsors.

Not everybody was happy to take on the responsibility. Henry Verney, who stood in for his brother Ralph at a family christening in 1655, wrote to Ralph afterwards with a disclaimer: 'For want of a godly godfather they invited my worshipp to stand, for wch in a word I did with a grave & religious grace; many promises I did make for you, such if you performe not, shall bee put on your score, in the next world, and not mine, for I doe as little love deepe and sollem ingagements, as your honour doth entringe into bonds.' Two centuries later Jane Welsh Carlyle was approached by a friend to be godmother to her daughter, but had too much integrity to accept:

> I should be greatly pleased that your baby bore a name of mine. But the Godmotherhood? There seems to me one objection to that, which is a fatal one – I don't belong to the English Church; and the Scotch Church, which I do belong to, recognises no Godfathers and Godmothers. . . . I was present at a Church of England christening for the first time, when the Blunts took me to see their baby christened, and it looked to me a very solemn piece of work; and that Mr. Maurice and Julia Blunt (the Godfather and Godmother) had to take upon themselves, before God and man, very solemn engagements, which it was to be hoped they meant to fulfil! I should not have liked to bow and murmur, and undertake all they did, without meaning to fulfil it according to my best ability. . . . I am not wanted to, it may perhaps be answered. . . . What are these spoken engagements then? A mere form; that is, a piece of humbug. How could I, in cold blood, go through with a ceremony in a church, to which neither the others nor myself attach a grain of veracity? If you can say anything to the purpose, I am very willing to be proved mistaken; and in that case very willing to stand Godmother to a baby that on the third day is not at all red!

At the baptism of illegitimate children, often the only way to procure godparents at all was to pay them. Thus in 1695 the parish authorities of

Birchington All Saints, Kent, 'paid for Gossipes for a poor travelling woman's child 3s0d',* and in Stockton, Shropshire, in 1784, a reluctant candidate had to be paid a shilling to stand godfather to 'Mary Rowley's base childe'.

The part traditionally played by the godparents at the ceremony itself was succinctly defined by one of the etiquette books: 'The chief godmother holds the baby during the earlier portion of the ceremony, standing at the clergyman's left hand; the nurse will be present also. . . . The godmother hands the child to the clergyman, and receives it from him again. When the time comes for naming the child, it is the godfather who has to reply to the clergyman's question.' Essentially this pattern has changed little, though some clergymen today make a point of actively involving all the godparents. In the Catholic ceremony the mother holds the baby herself.

The *Book of Common Prayer* explicitly requires godparents to ensure that their godchild 'may learn the Creed, the Lord's Prayer, and the Ten Commandments, in the vulgar tongue, and all other things which a Christian ought to know and believe to his soul's health; and that [he] may be virtuously brought up to lead a godly and a christian life'. *Debrett's Etiquette and Modern Manners* expresses the same idea in less specific terms: 'The duties of the godparents do not end with the ceremony and traditional christening gift. As the child grows, the link forged at baptism should become a bond; only the godparent can ensure that this occurs.' A charming example of this bond is afforded by the Moberlys. George Moberly was Headmaster of Winchester from 1835 to 1866, and Bishop of Salisbury from 1869. His was a large family, and after the baptism of his youngest child in 1854 he wrote in his diary: 'And so I have fifteen little Christians of my own to guard and guide as a father may.' With such a constant succession of christenings, it is not surprising that they evolved into a traditional ritual. A great crowd of friends always attended, and everybody walked together from the Headmaster's house to the chapel, each Moberly child who had not yet been con-

---

* Gossipes = godmothers. James Melville, the envoy of Mary Queen of Scots to the court of Queen Elizabeth, noted that 'I requested Her Majesty [Elizabeth] to be a gossip to the Queen [i.e. godmother to Prince James], for our *cummers* are called *gossips* in England; to which she gladly condescended.' My italics. The word *cummer* is a variation of the French *commère*, which initially meant a fellow godparent, and now means a gossip.

firmed being escorted by his or her godparents, a public manifestation of the continuing bond. But less godly parents than the Moberlys were more likely to feel with Dickens's Mr Dombey that any interest in the child's future spiritual life was an unwarranted interference:

> During the whole of these proceedings, Mr. Dombey remained as impassive and gentlemanly as ever, and perhaps assisted in making it so cold, that the young curate smoked at the mouth as he read. The only time that he unbent his visage in the least was when the clergyman, in delivering (very unaffectedly and simply) the closing exhortation, relative to the future examination of the child by the sponsors, happened to rest his eye on Mr. Chick; and then Mr. Dombey might have been seen to express, by a majestic look, that he would like to catch him at it. . . .

When by force of circumstance a proper church christening was not possible, mothers were forced to improvise. Medieval layfolk may have been instructed in the proper form of baptism, but later generations were not, and had either to risk a long delay or fall back on memory or imagination. Several Australian ballads concern the unavailability of clergymen to do the job, and although they are humorous in tone, it was clearly a very real problem. In J. Brunton Stephens's tragicomic *Drought and Doctrine* the narrator recalls:

> So, when our last began to pine, an' lost his pretty smile,
> An' not a parson to be had within a hunder mile –
> (For though there is chapel down at Bluegrass Creek, you know,
> The clergy's there on dooty only thrice a year or so) –
> Well, when our yet unchristened mite grew limp an' thin an' pale,
> It would 'a cut you to the heart to hear the mother wail
> About her 'unregenerate babe', an' how, if it should go,
> 'Twould have no chance with them as had their registers to show.

Hardy's Tess, similarly anguished at the prospect of her illegitimate baby dying unbaptized and being consigned to Hell, determined to do the job herself:

Pulling out the washing-stand so that she could get behind it, she poured some water from a jug, and made [her brothers and sisters] kneel around, putting their hands together with fingers exactly vertical. . . . Tess then stood erect with the infant on her arm beside the basin, the next sister held the Prayer-Book open before her, as the clerk at church held it before the parson; and thus the girl set about baptizing her child.

And when the following morning the baby dies,

> . . . the calmness which had possessed Tess since the christening remained with her in the infant's loss. In the daylight, indeed, she felt her terrors about his soul to have been somewhat exaggerated; whether well founded or not she had no uneasiness now, reasoning that if Providence would not ratify such an act of approximation, she, for one, did not value the kind of heaven lost by the irregularity – either for herself or for her child.

A happier example of an improvised christening is afforded by Martha Martin, in her autobiographical book *O Rugged Land of Gold* (1953). Martha and her husband were gold prospectors in Alaska, and after a landslide separated them she was left to see the winter through in their cabin, completely alone, with several bones broken, and pregnant. She lived through it all, kept a diary, had her baby, and when spring came she was reunited with her husband. Despite, or perhaps because of, her total isolation, she was determined to keep up all the traditions of civilized life, and so she decided to have a christening party for her baby girl, although it would be very different from the one her son had had:

> Lloyd was christened in Epiphany Church; Donnas will be christened by the side of the sea. All our friends and relatives came to see Lloyd baptized. Many friends will come to see Donnas baptized, but no relatives will be there, no godparents. Many deer will come, perhaps the ravens will fly over, the jays will be on hand, and a great eagle might look on from a far-off high perch.

Martha had no prayer-book to follow, so she made up a service herself from her own memories of being a godmother:

> Donnas was dressed in all her finery and wrapped in the otter robe, only her little face showing deep down in the fur. She was so good, wiggling just a little, making small grunts, her little eyes open part of the time, peeping out now and then to see the vastness of the world where she has come to dwell. I carried her proudly to the water's edge, scattered food about, and waited for the deer to come.
>
> 'Dearly beloved,' I told my baby and the assembled crowd, 'we are gathered together here in the sight of God and in the face of this company to baptize this child, that she may be baptized with water and the Holy Spirit and be received into the spiritual fellowship of the kingdom of God and become a member of the same. Almighty and everlasting God, heavenly Father, Lord God of Hosts, we give Thee thanks for all Thy many blessings, the greatest and best of which is the placing of this child in our care. O God, grant that this child may be endowed with heavenly virtues and blessed through Thy mercy. This I ask through Jesus Christ our Lord, to whom be all honour and glory, now and forever. Amen.'
>
> Then I knelt down at the edge of the sea and said:
>
> 'Donnas Martin, I baptize thee in the name of the Father, and of the Son, and of the Holy Ghost. Amen.'
>
> I dipped the tips of my fingers in the water and signed my child with the sign of the Cross . . .
>
> Donnas did not cry at the cold water, didn't even whimper. She is a well-mannered little lady. I continued with the christening service.
>
> 'Defend, O Lord, this my child,' I said, still kneeling, 'with Thy heavenly grace. Keep her in paths of righteousness for Thy name's sake, and at last bring her into Thy everlasting kingdom.'
>
> Then I said the Lord's Prayer, and Baby and I went back to the cabin.

2

FOLKLORE

One for sorrow,
Two for mirth,
Three for a wedding,
Four for a birth.

Magpies, old English rhyme

The acceptance of Christianity has never precluded adherence to older beliefs and customs; rather, Christianity and paganism have maintained an uneasy coexistence. It is easy to see why. Nations or communities have usually become Christian in the wake, or at the command, of a particular leader: events such as Iceland's wholesale conversion in AD 1000 took little account of personal conviction. When Charlemagne carried out his mass baptisms of Saxons by the simple expedient of driving them into the river at sword-point while one of his bishops stood upstream blessing the waters as they flowed past the 'converts', the Saxons took the precaution of keeping their sword arms out of the water in order to preserve their pagan vigour. This practice, we are told, continued among the Irish into the sixteenth century. Thus Christianity was seen as a competitor to paganism, not as a refutation of it, and the common people hedged their bets by keeping a foot firmly in both camps.

The Church insisted that those who died unbaptized could not go to Heaven, and therefore urged early baptism. (There was some dispute as to where they did go, some claiming with St Augustine that they were doomed to perpetual punishment, others, like Thomas Aquinas, that they went to Limbo where they enjoyed full natural happiness, but not supernatural beatitude.) This was the logical outcome of the belief in original sin, whereby the whole of mankind is held to be innately corrupt as a result of Adam's fall. Thus even new-born babies are technically in a state of sin, from which only baptism can cleanse them. Folk belief was equally adamant that the unbaptized could enjoy no rest, and many different fates were supposed to await them. In Manx lore they were condemned to wander for ever, carrying a light (the story of the Child of Eary Cushlin is told in Chapter 3); in Devon they joined the Yeth Hounds who hunt over the moor with the Devil; in Somerset the restless spirit fluttered about as a 'spunky' and appeared as a will-o'-the-wisp, or became a moth; in Nidderdale it was a nightjar; elsewhere a butterfly; and in many areas it was thought to join the fairies. A similar belief in the restlessness and malevolence of unbaptized souls is found in parts of Africa. In some communities children who die unnamed cannot be interred for fear of offending the Earth shrines which represent Life and Fertility. Among the Lodagaa of Ghana they are buried under a mound of earth at a crossroads, the cradle being placed on top of the mound with a stake through it to prevent the child from returning to haunt its parents. The Nigerian Yorubas believe that these children roam around in gangs by night, and they hold special feasts to appease them.

The graves of unbaptized children were traditionally considered unlucky. Anyone who had the temerity to tread on such 'unchristened ground' was certain to be afflicted with grave-merels or grave-scab, a fatal disease that produced trembling of the limbs and hard breathing, and a sensation as though the skin were being touched with hot iron.

While the influence of the fairy world was, in popular belief, ever present, it was at its strongest over those – either newly born or on the brink of death – who were near the confluence of two worlds. Baptism was the surest protection from the fairies' sinister intentions, and until it had been administered the child was at risk. Witches were thought to seek an unbaptized infant's fat for their spells, and Walpurgis night, the eve of 1 May, when they held their Sabbath, was particularly dangerous on this account. The Greeks and Slavs believed that the Lamia had power over such a child, and innumerable folk-tales testify to the fear that it might be stolen away by fairies. Certain precautions were essential to avert this threat. The child must not be taken into a strange house, nor must anyone walk between its cradle and the fire. The mother's bed

From a fourteenth-century manuscript

could be 'sained' by carrying a lighted torch or candle round it. Salt, garlic, a branch of rowan or a piece of iron could be placed in the cradle, or it could be hung with scarlet rags or ribbons, for fairies were thought to fear the colour red. In the Isle of Man soot was smeared on the baby's arm, and if the mother had to leave the room for any reason she crossed the tongs and poker over the cradle. In Germany it was guarded by snapdragon or horehound, blue marjoram, black cumin, a right shirt-sleeve and a left stocking. In Scotland the child was protected by an article of its father's clothing, and in his *Folklore of the Northern Counties of England and the Borders* William Henderson records a chilling tale to this effect:

This was experienced by the wife of a shepherd near Selkirk. Soon after the birth of her first child, a fine boy, she was lying in bed with her baby by her side, when suddenly she became aware of a confused noise of talking and merry laughter in the 'spence', or room. This, in fact, proceeded from the fairies, who were forming a child of wax as a substitute for the baby, which they were planning to steal away. The poor mother suspected as much, so in great alarm she seized her husband's waistcoat,which chanced to be lying at the foot of the bed, and flung it over herself and the child. The fairies set up a loud scream, calling out 'Auld lucky has cheated us o' our bairnie!' Soon afterwards the woman heard something fall down the lum (or chimney), and looking out she saw a waxen image of her baby, stuck full of pins, lying on the hearth. When her husband came home he made up a large fire and threw the fairy lump upon it; but instead of burning, the thing flew up the chimney, and the house instantly resounded with shouts of joy and peals of laughter.

A Manx story on the same theme illustrates very clearly the coexistence of Christian and pagan beliefs. Here again a woman was lying in bed with her new-born baby when two very old women suddenly burst through the door and came up to the bed, where they grabbed hold of the child and tried to take it away, one of them urging 'Gow ee, gow ee!' ('Take her, take her') and the other replying 'Cha jargym, cha jargym!' ('I can't, I can't!') In the tussle that ensued they upset a jug of water which was standing by the bedside and the mother called out 'Jee jean myghin orrym!' ('God have mercy on me!') Immediately the old women dropped the baby and ran for it, but although she grew up and lived to a ripe old age she always retained the fairies' finger-marks on her heel.

The Welsh have many stories of changelings left by the fairies when they stole human babies. In her book *Crafts, Customs and Legends of Wales* Mary Corbett Harris recalls that

> . . . as a child in Merioneth, I was told the frightening story of a human baby stolen many years ago from a cottage near my home and of the dreadful little 'plentyn-newydd' left in its place by the fairies. After many difficulties the mother found where the baby had been hidden, and managed to rescue it. I have often trudged up the steep path winding through the dark trees along which she is supposed to have dashed, her baby in her arms, the fairies in hot pursuit.

Thus baptism was sought after for much more than its strictly orthodox significance. There was a very widespread belief that a child could never thrive until it had been christened, and that baptism could actually effect a cure in a weak or ailing child. (This belief is paralleled among the Lapps, where the baptism and naming ceremony may be repeated any number of times in case of illness, in order to defeat the evil spirit that is causing the trouble.) In 1838 the Revd Archer Clive recorded in his diary: 'I went to call at Overley where I had been summoned the evening before to baptize a sick child. The poor mother said she thought Baptism always made a great change and that the child either speedily grew better or worse. In this case it was certainly better but I told her that God gave no such promise with regard to health of body.'

Nevertheless the belief persisted. In the 1860s the story was noted of a chimney-sweep's sickly child who appeared to be on the point of death. A neighbour inquired whether it had been baptized, and on learning that it had not, said, 'I would try having it christened.' This was done and the child recovered. Twenty years later still, the Rector of Dorstone in Herefordshire noted that his parishioners brought their babies to him as a last resort when they were ailing, saying: 'The child won't take nothing, don't aim to such at all, and seems always wantin', and we've tried it with potato and fat pork and all, but can't satisfy it no-way, and gran'mer says, "Go to the Reverend," her says, "and beg of him to christen it, 'twill be all right then."'

In a very natural process of transition, the baptismal water itself came to be credited with physical as well as spiritual properties. In the Middle Ages Copts and Muslims participated in a baptismal river festival in the Nile on the eve of Epiphany, which was held to cure all illnesses. Many sects in the United States hold group baptisms in rivers, and Primitive Baptists there believe that this can never lead to the participants' catching cold, no matter how chilly the day or how freezing the water. (When he played the part of John the Baptist in *The Greatest Story Ever Told*, Charlton Heston had to spend several November days standing waist-deep in the Colorado River. Afterwards he commented: 'If the River Jordan had been as cold as the Colorado, Christianity would never have got off the ground.' It is all a matter of faith.) Baptismal water was much in demand for its healing properties. It could be administered as medicine, or a weak child might be bathed in it, and it was universally considered unlucky to wipe away what was left on the child's forehead after the ceremony. In the middle of the last century the old monthly nurse of Churchdown, in Gloucestershire, rinsed out the infant's mouth with the water left from the christening, and assured the vicar that this would prevent toothache. In Wales the water left in the font was thrown out into the garden, preferably over the leek-bed. In the Orkneys it was doubly precious because only fresh spring water, called Wild Water, was used, and this was thought to have magical properties in its own right. But the water was also sought for sinister purposes connected with witchcraft. To prevent any such malpractice, Bishop Quevil ruled, at the Synod of Exeter in 1287, that when a child had been baptized at home the remaining water should either be thrown on the fire or brought to church and there poured down the 'sacrarium'; and fonts in churches frequently had locked covers so that the water could not be stolen.

In Germany it was thought that a child who cried at its christening would not live to grow old, but in Britain some kind of protest was generally considered a good thing. The most widespread belief was that the crying represented the Devil being driven out, though on the Welsh border, more prosaically, it was thought to be an indication that the child would grow up with a fine singing voice. The cry was also thought to symbolize the pangs of the new birth, and some people believed that a child who failed to cry was showing that it was too good to live. In 1842 Caroline Clive noted in her diary: 'On the 16th our boy was christened. . . . The ceremony was performed after the morning service and he cried only enough to satisfy his nurse who said she must have pinched him if he had been totally silent because children who don't cry when christened die soon after.'

When the high rate of infant mortality made early, and even same-day baptism a necessity, many of the customs and rituals pertaining to birth extended to the christening as well. Both events attracted large numbers of people to the house, so that supplies had to be laid in for their sustenance. In most areas the food provided was cheese and either bread or cake, from the spicy pepper-cake of Yorkshire to the currant-studded 'cheeld's fuggan' of Cornwall. Both cheese and cake were good keepers, and could therefore be prepared well in advance, though in England this was not taken to such extremes as in Sweden: there the food was placed in bed with the bride on her wedding night, though whether this practice suggests an advanced degree of domestic organization and forethought, or merely a high incidence of last-minute weddings, would be hard to say. At any rate the food served to sustain the helpers and the flagging father either during, or immediately after, the birth, at what was somewhat inaptly called the Merry Meal. (The cake, in deference to the main participant in the drama, was sometimes called the groaning-cake.) In Oxfordshire a curious ritual took place whereby the pieces served at the Merry Meal were cut from the middle of the cake, which left the outer edge in the shape of a ring, and through this ring the baby was passed on the christening day in what was clearly a symbolic re-enactment of the birth process.

A gift of food was one way of disarming the evil influences that were lying in wait for the unbaptized child. This is one reason for the very

Font *c.* 1000, Melbury Bubb, Dorset

widespread custom of taking food along to the christening and offering it to the first-comer. In County Durham cake and cheese left over from the Merry Meal were offered to the first person encountered who was of the opposite sex to the baby. In south Somerset any stranger was offered bread and cheese, but had to give a penny in return in order to secure good fortune for the child. The coin was kept as a lucky token. In the Isle of Man 'blithe meat' or *arran as caashey* – bread and cheese – was given unconditionally to all-comers. A certain man from Kirk Maughold known as Ned Lag y Thurran (Ned of the Hollow of the Stack) from his habit of sleeping in haystacks, capitalized on this tradition and used to lie in wait on the road to the church to claim his bread and cheese from any passing christening party. A Devon squire described the same custom to the *Western Morning News* in 1883:

> I was driving the other day, when on passing a market trap, I suddenly had a cake thrust into my hand, amidst shouts of 'The Squire has get 'en'. I said, 'Really I am much obliged, but I do not want it.' 'Oh, but you must have it; it is the christening cake', was the rejoinder, shouted out by the now passing occupants of the trap. After they had driven on, I asked my coachman (who has lived in the parish a full forty years), whether he could explain the matter; and he told me that, 'the cake was given to the first person that was met by a christening party on the way to church'. I accordingly gave the cake to him, as he was on the box, and therefore was clearly entitled to it. He was delighted; he said, 'I've heard tell of the custom all my life, but this is the first time I have ever met with it.'

The publication of this story led many people to write to the paper with accounts of similar experiences. The custom seems to have been most tenacious in Cornwall. One correspondent described the scene at his brother's christening some thirty years earlier (i.e. in the 1850s):

> When the family party was ready for the walk to the afternoon service in Cury church, I well recollect seeing the old nurse wrap in a pure white sheet of paper what she called the 'cheeld's fuggan'. This was a cake with plenty of currants and saffron, about the size of a modern

tea-plate. It was to be given to the first person met on returning, after the child was christened. It happened that, as most of the parishioners were at the service, no one was met until near home, almost a mile from the church, when a tipsy village carpenter rambled around a corner, right against our party, and received the cake. Regrets were expressed that the 'cheeld's fuggan' should have fallen to the lot of this notoriously evil liver, and my idea was that it was a bad omen. However as my brother has always been a veritable Rechabite, enjoys good health, a contented mind, and enough of this world's goods to satisfy every moderate want, no evil can thus far be traced to the mischance.

The 'cheeld's fuggan' of western Cornwall was known as the 'kimbly' in eastern parts and the 'christening-crib' in the south-east. When the writer Kenneth Grahame stood godfather to the son of American friends at Fowey in 1907 they duly observed the custom, though this may have been a deliberately nostalgic gesture. But as late as 1932 a case was recorded in St Ives of a biscuit being offered to the first person encountered on the way by a christening party bound for church.

One way of ensuring long life for the baby was to ask the first poor person encountered on the way to church to be its godparent. On the other hand if a pregnant woman stood as godmother, either her own child or her godchild would die prematurely. Queen Victoria had clearly never come across this belief, and therefore dismissed it as foreign nonsense when she wrote to her daughter Vicky, who had married the Crown Prince of Prussia:

Of all the wonderful German notions that one of a lady in your condition being unable to stand godmother is the most extraordinary I ever heard! Is a woman really bewitched or possessed to be considered unlucky? I think that must be only a Prussian notion (perhaps Russian?) because I have heard of so many christenings abroad where people have been in that condition and stand as godmothers. I hope that you will break through that. . . .

In parts of Cornwall it was thought that if a young man and woman were godparents to the same child they were certain to become sweethearts;

but on the other hand a couple from Penzance refused the honour on grounds of ill luck, saying 'First at the font, never at the altar'. This may have been a throw-back to a dimly recollected article of Canon Law, which ruled that co-sponsorship was one of the prohibited degrees of affinity.

Throughout the north of England and Scotland it was believed that if boys and girls were brought to baptism together, the boys must go first, otherwise they would grow up to be effeminate while the girls would be mannish. The north door of the church was left open during the ceremony so that the Devil could make his escape through it. If one of the godparents looked into the font the child would grow up to look like him or her. Caroline Clive noted as 'another unlucky sign' at her son's christening the fact that the godmother was in mourning. In Northumberland the child kept on the little cap he had worn at the ceremony until the morning of the following day. A mid-Victorian vicar noted that

> . . . loud murmurs arose against me, early in my ministerial life, for applying so much water that the cap had to be taken off and dried, whereas it should be left on till the next morning. I threw the blame on the modern caps with their expanse of frilling, on which the good woman said that I was quite right; she had an old christening cap, the heirloom of a friend, which she could show me, of a very different make. Accordingly I examined the cap, which was evidently very old, and made with reference to affusion in baptism. It excluded forehead, ears, and chin, and apparently never had strings. I said that if a mother would bring her baby in such a cap, I would undertake not to wet it.

Nearer our own time, in North America, Martha Martin recorded (and indulged in) a local superstition. When she had completed the christening ceremony for her baby daughter Donnas, 'right quick, I looked to see if she had wet her diaper. She had not; and that was a sure sign, so the old folks say, that all the days of her life she will be upright and worthy, a person of honour and integrity, loved and respected by all who know her'.

Towards the end of the nineteenth century, when urban life was bringing increased sophistication even to country areas, many of the old customs and beliefs began to fall into disuse even as they were being enthusiastically recorded by folklorists. This transitional stage is beautifully captured by Flora Thompson in *Still Glides the Stream*. It is little Polly's christening, and gauche, unsophisticated Luke has been asked to be godfather:

Once or twice Luke put out his big hand and touched the tiny fingers of his godchild. Since the demand for roasted chestnuts had slacked he had become thoughtful. He opened his mouth as though about to speak, then closed it again and fidgeted with some coins in his pocket. His silence and unease became so marked that Charity's father exclaimed, 'Why, Luke, what ails you, man? You've been fidgeting this last ten minutes like a cat on hot bricks. If you've got anything to say, out with it!' and, thus brought to the point, Luke dipped into the pocket with which he had been concerned and brought out a sixpence which he deposited upon the little round chimney-corner table beside Mrs. Truman.

'A sixpence! A bright and shining new sixpence!' she said, raising her eyebrows, 'But why? And what for?'

'For her,' stammered Luke nervously, indicating the baby. 'To – to wet her hair and to bring her good luck.' His elders gazed at him in silence for a moment. They were in a delicate position. Luke's offering was a considerable amount out of his small spending-money and it could not be refused without hurting his feelings. Yet, on the other hand, they all, except Reuben, prided themselves upon belonging to a new and unsuperstitious generation which abominated such old heathenish practices as wetting the head of a newly-born child with spirits. Charity's mother especially objected to the custom still observed in the village of wetting a child's head with gin immediately after its christening; before, as she said, the blessed water was dry on its forehead.

They stared in silence at Luke, and he, never dreaming that any objection could exist to a custom observed by his parents and grandparents, and relieved that he had fulfilled his last duty as a godfather, without, as he had said, making a fool of himself, beamed back upon them. Then Mrs. Truman took up the sixpence – she said afterwards that it was nearly red hot from his constant handling – and said warmly: 'That's real good of you, Luke, and 'twill bring little Polly good luck, I feel certain. But, myself, I haven't much faith in the gin, and she does so badly need a pair of little woolly bootikins to keep her tootsies warm, so, if you're sure you don't mind, I'll get her a pair with your sixpence next time I go shopping and you shall come in and put them on for her the first time of wearing. What colour would you like me to get, pink or pale blue?' Luke turned to Bess for advice as to colour and the episode ended happily. Soon afterwards the christening party broke up.

3

NAMES

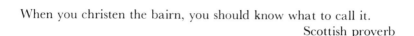

When you christen the bairn, you should know what to call it.

Scottish proverb

From Africa to Polynesia, among North American Indians and Lapps, the naming of a baby is combined with a ceremony of initiation or presentation. Jewish boys receive their name when they are circumcized into the Covenant on the eighth day of life, and girls when their father is called to the Torah on the Sabbath following their birth. Muslim children are usually named on the seventh day: the father recites verses from the Koran in the presence of family and friends and then announces the name, after which there is a feast. Sikh children are named when they are presented before Guru Granth Sahib. The Granth is opened at random and the first letter of the first hymn on that page becomes the child's initial. Names are not given exclusively at the beginning of physical life, but also to mark a new beginning or the assumption of a new identity. Early converts to Christianity took a new name to symbolize their spiritual rebirth; monks and nuns are renamed when they take their vows; Roman Catholics add on an extra name at confirmation to show that they are embarking on spiritual adulthood; and in the Western secular world it is not uncommon to adopt a new name at the outset of a career, particularly in show business.

In primitive belief a person's name is in a very real sense a part of him, and there are certain societies where it is unlucky for the name ever to be revealed, people going by nicknames all their lives in the belief that to know a man's name is to have power over him. In Icelandic saga the name of a dead relative given to a child carried with it some of the first owner's personality, and afforded him a kind of reincarnation. A further

51

corollary to the belief that name and personality are intimately connected is the feeling that until it has a name a child is not a complete
person and therefore has no rights. In ancient Norse custom a father was
entitled to expose his children until such time as they had under-
gone the naming ceremony, or *vatni ausa*, but once they had a name
and an official identity they were protected by the law. In English
tradition it has always been thought unlucky to tell anyone a child's
name, or indeed to use it at all, before the christening. As late as 1971
a Cambridge woman told an interviewer that she and her husband had
discussed possible names for their baby, but had publicly referred to him
by a nickname until such time as he was 'safely baptized'.

To die unbaptized has always been considered of the gravest import
on both theological and superstitious grounds. In Flora Thompson's *Still
Glides the Stream*, Charity learns that her uncle's first wife Lavinia 'had
been buried with a little day-old baby on her arm which could not be
mentioned on the headstone because it had not been baptized', the clear
implication being that the poor nameless child did not count as a real
person; and the Manx folk-tale of the Child of Eary Cushlin makes it
quite plain that the lack of a name was the heaviest part of the
unbaptized child's burden. The heiress of Eary Cushlin Farm had an
illegitimate child which died soon after birth. The mother buried it at
dead of night on the hillside overlooking the waters of Lag-ny-Killey,
and told no one. But soon afterwards the men fishing in the area noticed
a light moving about on the hill and heard the sound of a child crying,
night after night, and they became so frightened that they refused to go
out into the bay after dark:

> Things became so black for the women and children at home that one
> old, old man, Illiam Quirk, who had not gone to sea for many years,
> said he would go with one of the yawls to see for himself. They used to
> say of him: 'Oul Illiam has the power at him in the prayer, and he is a
> middlin' despard fella; he will dar' most anything.' It was so at this
> time – his yawl was the last of them coming in; the rest were
> frightened. It was a right fine, beautiful moonlight night when he was
> coming down from the mark, and when he was near to Gob-yn-
> Ushtey he heard crying and crying. He lay on his oars and listened,
> and he heard a little child wailing over and over again: 'She lhiannoo

beg dyn ennym mee!' That is, 'I am a little child without a name!'

'Pull nearer to the lan',' said Illiam when he heard it. They pulled close in, and he plainly saw a little child on the strand bearing a lighted candle in its hand.

'God bless me, bogh, we mus' give thee a name!' said Illiam. And he took off his hat, and stood up in the boat, and threw a handful of water towards the child, crying out: 'If thou are a boy, I chrizzen thee in the name of the Father, Son, and Holy Ghost, Juan! If thou are a girl I chrizzen thee in the name of the Father, Son, and Holy Ghost, Joanney!'

In an instant the crying stopped, and was never heard again, and the light went out and was seen no more.

There are many superstitions and customs regarding names. In Yugoslavia it was traditional to give a boy two names in order to ensure long life. In Herefordshire it is thought lucky if the child's initials spell a complete name, but unlucky to name a child after a favourite animal. The story is told of a baby girl who was named after her father's favourite mare; she died at the age of three and the mare fell and broke her neck not long after. Some people believe that a dead child will come and call away any subsequent child of the same name (though in the days of large families and high infant mortality names were frequently repeated). Christina Hole remembers a farm labourer whose baby, Joseph, died. He called the next child Joseph as well, and he died too. Both parents were convinced that the first child had 'called him to himself'. If they believed this could happen, one wonders what induced them to put the second child thus at risk. At Buckland Newton, in Dorset, it was the custom to name all the children of a family by the same initial. One labourer with a large family, when names beginning with M ran short, was driven to call two of his daughters Mehetabel and Mahalath.

On the whole a baby's name is chosen by its parents, not always without disagreement. Ralph and Mary Verney, a most devoted couple, separated for a time during the Civil War, carried on quite an argument in their letters about the name of the child Mary was expecting. 'Richard is a good name for a boy,' wrote Ralph, 'and your owne for a girle, but let it not bee Susan's, Thomas' nor my owne I charge you.'

Mary, however, had her own ideas: 'If itt be a boy I am resollved to have itt of thy owne name, therefore I charge you doe nott contredict itt; but if itt be a gerle I leave it wholly to thee to chuse. . . . I will be governed by thee in anything but the name if it be a boy, for to tell the truth I must have itt have thy name.' Ralph persisted: 'Now for the name. If it bee a girle and that you have noe conceit because the other died, I desire it may bee Mary; but if it bee a boy, in earnest you must not deny mee, let it bee Richard or what you please, except my owne name. Really I shall take it ill if you contradict mee in this.' Mary had her baby on 3 June 1647, and it was a boy. Ralph made a last bid: 'If the boye's name is Richard I shall hope he may bee a happy man; but if it bee otherwise I will not prophecie his ill-fortune, but rather pray to God to make him an honest man, and then he will be happy enough.' But Mary, doubtless fearful of never seeing her beloved husband again, and wanting a living reminder of him, did call the baby Ralph, at which her husband pretended great anger: 'I will not now dispute with you about his name, but assure your selfe you shall heare of it at large heerafter.' We can only assume that in the rapture of reunion the argument was abandoned and Mary forgiven.

The Vicar of Wakefield was another father who found himself overruled in the matter of names: 'Our second child, a girl, I intended to call after her aunt Grissel; but my wife, who during her pregnancy had been reading romances, insisted upon her being called Olivia.' He clearly stood for many others, for a century later a writer in *London Society* who was bemoaning the whole tedious and expensive business of having children complained that 'the British Paterfamilias generally respects the memory of his great-aunt and grandmother, and is willing enough to call [his daughter] Susan or Jane. But the mother is rather like the Vicar of Wakefield's wife, who read novels when she was laid up and selected the fine name of the heroine'.

Many people, however, believed that the godparents had the right to choose the name. The good Vicar complained that on the birth of his second daughter, 'I was determined that Grissel should be her name; but a rich relation taking a fancy to stand godmother, the girl was, by her directions, called Sophia: so that we had two romantic names in the family; but I solemnly protest I had no hand in it.' Charlotte M. Yonge was more diffident about suggesting a name when asked to be godmother to the youngest daughter of her friends the Moberlys, in 1852: 'Indeed I do thank you and Mrs. Moberly very much for giving me a pearl to think of every day. I should like for her to be Margaret Helen, though as it is for the sake of nothing but some fancies of my own it does not deserve to be twice thought about.' Her wish was respected and Margaret Helen was the name given the baby. The Vicar of Glynde on the other hand positively insisted that the godparents should choose his children's names for him. On one occasion, 'when de St. Croix said, "Name this child", the Godmother looked at the Godfathers, they looked at her; all had forgotten to inquire what name the parents wished. They asked Mr. de St. Croix, "It is your business to choose the name," he rejoined. The Godmother suggested "William" . . . . "It is already the name of one of my children." A second name was suggested and the same answer. At the third name the father baptized the child'.

But sometimes godparents abused their privilege. One vicar recalled a baptism where the godmother, when asked to name the child, started off with Arabella and worked right through the alphabet with the longest names she could think up. When asked afterwards whatever she had done such a thing for, she retorted that it was to spite the parents, as she had not wished to be godmother in the first place.

In France a revolutionary law still in operation decrees that the only names that may be used are those which have been taken from the calendars of saints or from ancient history. In Germany no name may be given unless it can be established that it has been used before. In Great Britain, as in the United States, parents are free to call their children whatever they please, though sometimes they may not get their first choice if the minister exercises his right of veto. An amusing instance was recounted to the Vicar of East Dereham at the end of the nineteenth century. A father presented his son for baptism, wishing to call him by the shortest name in the Bible, Uz. The minister objected; whereupon the father, who either had an encyclopedic knowledge of the Bible or had anticipated this turn of events, retorted, 'Well, if he cannot have the shortest he shall have the longest', and proceeded to name him Mahershallalashbaz.* Another, more celebrated, instance of

*This name was not unknown among the Puritans of New England, prompting the author of *American Given Names* to speculate as to how it might have been shortened for everyday use. He suggests Hash or Buzz.

veto occurred at the christening of the child who later became
Queen Victoria. The proposed names, Georgiana Charlotte Augusta
Alexandrina Victoria (Alexandrina in honour of Tsar Alexander I of
Russia, one of the godfathers), were submitted for the approval of her
uncle the Prince Regent, who was to be the other godfather. The evening
before the ceremony he announced that Georgiana was out of the
question, 'as He did not chuse to place His name before the Emperor of
Russia's – and He could not allow it to follow'. The other names he would
discuss at the christening. When the time came, and the names were put
forward, he kept silent for a long time. At last he grudgingly allowed
Alexandrina to pass, but angrily vetoed both Charlotte and Augusta.
Finally, when urged to suggest a second name, he scowled at his sister-
in-law, who was by now in tears, and snapped, 'Let her be called after
her mother', and so she became Alexandrina Victoria.

Occasionally parents were done out of the name of their choice by a
straightforward mistake. When babies frequently died either during, or
immediately after, birth, midwives were trained to perform emergency
baptism, sometimes during labour itself. In these cases a girl might
get a boy's name or vice versa, the midwife having been too agitated
to check the sex properly, or having administered the rite before it could
be known. Because of this hazard, children baptized in this way were
sometimes given a neutral name, the favourite being Creatura Christi or
just plain Creature. But it was not only the strain of a difficult birth that
could cause mistakes. The parish records of Bishop Wearmouth in
County Durham contain the entry: *Robert, daughter of William Thompson,
bap. 15 Feb. 1730, the midwife mistaking the sex, – she was crazed with liquor.*

Although Carola Oman's parents chose her name themselves, they
were soon disenchanted with it. As noted earlier, she was baptized in the
chapel of All Souls College in 1897, and after the ceremony one of the
Fellows suggested that, as she was the first child to enjoy this privilege,
she might have been named Anima. Her parents, who clearly had a
penchant for unusual names, as they had called their elder daughter
Dulce, after the school song of Winchester, asked indignantly why he
had not mentioned this idea before, as they would certainly have acted
on it. The professor rather diffidently confessed that he had once before
ventured to suggest a name for a christening, and that 'it was not at all
cordially received'. It was too late for the disappointed parents to do

anything about it, but they did not give up the idea, and in 1914 their daughter was confirmed as Carola Mary Anima.

Theoretically British parents have always enjoyed freedom of choice where names are concerned, but in practice they have been restricted by convention and the desire to please friends or relatives. In the past it was usual for the first son and daughter to be given the name of their father and mother, but thereafter the choice was wider. Of the numerous babies whom John Evelyn saw christened, a substantial number were named after grandparents (as was he). Indeed there is an almost apologetic entry for 19 May 1698 when he notes the christening of his grandson William Draper: 'They would faine have had it Evelyn (making me Godfather as I was) but for some reasons I desired it might be William.' Very frequently the child was called after one of the godparents (as opposed to the godparent choosing the name), a situation that called for much tact, since each child had two godparents of its own sex. In 1661 Pepys stood godfather to Sir William Batten's nephew, and took a suitably handsome gift along to the christening, 'but for as much I expected to give the name to the child, but did not (it being called John), I forebore then to give my plate till another time after more advice'. Sometimes more than a present was at stake. In Trollope's *Is He Popenjoy?* a rich relative offers £20,000 to a financially embarrassed couple on consideration of becoming godmother to their baby:

There was a strong opposition to Miss Tallowax's liberal offer; but, in the end, it was accepted. The £20,000 was important; and, after all, the godmother could do no lasting injury to the child. Then it was discovered that the offer was clogged with a further stipulation. The boy must be christened Tallowax! To this father and mother and aunts all objected, swearing that they would not subject their young Popenjoy to so great an injury – till it was ascertained that the old lady did not insist on Tallowax as a first name, or even as a second. It would suffice that Tallowax should be inserted among others. It was at last decided that the boy should be christened Frederic Augustus Tallowax. Thus he became Frederic Augustus Tallowax Germain, commonly to be called, by the queen's courtesy, Lord Popenjoy.

Recently (January 1986) a correspondent wrote to *The Times* with a

list of names, common a century ago and now obsolete, and concluded
his letter with the question, 'Did any one know a Kerenhappuch?'
From the many replies it emerged that the name had indeed been in use
a hundred or so years ago, and one of the correspondents recounted that
he had had a great-aunt of that name who had promised a legacy should
a particular child be called after her. The mother could not bring herself
to inflict the whole name on her daughter, and compromised with
Keren, a reluctance that lost the child the legacy.

The parents' choice of names is also heavily influenced by fashion.
Thus in the Middle Ages children were almost invariably called after
saints. After the Reformation these names lost their popularity and only
biblical names found favour. And the Puritans, wishing to set themselves
apart from the supposedly godless masses, turned to qualities and
precepts – Sorry-for-Sin, or the celebrated Praisegod Barebones and
Preserved Fish. In the eighteenth century there was a trend among all
classes for less edifying and more fanciful names. The poet Crabbe made
gentle fun of the pretensions of simple folk in his *Parish Register* (1807):

> But I digress, and lo! an infant train
> Appear, and call me to my task again.
> 'Why Lonicera wilt thou name thy child?'
> I ask'd the Gardener's wife, in accents mild:
> 'We have a right,' replied the sturdy dame; –
> And Lonicera was the infant's name.
> If next a son shall yield our Gardener joy,
> Then Hyacinthus shall be that fair boy;
> And if a girl, they will at length agree,
> That Belladonna that fair maid shall be. . . .
> Pride lives with all; strange names our rustics give
> To helpless infants, that their own may live;
> Pleased to be known, they'll some attention claim,
> And find some by-way to the house of fame.

Queen Victoria, by her blameless morals and her commitment to
family life, effectively redeemed the monarchy from the odium which
the Hanoverians had provoked. She and Albert, with their large brood
of children, represented a beau ideal of domesticity for her subjects up

and down the land, and the names they bore no less than the clothes they wore set instant fashions. John Leech drew a cartoon for *Punch* entitled 'Maternal Solicitude' which shows two middle-class women in conversation. The caption reads: 'And the dear children?' 'Why, Alexandrina Victoria is a good deal better; but dear little Albert here is still very delicate.' Edith Nesbit was laughing at the same fashion in *Five Children and It* (1902) when she called the children of Lady Chittenden's coachman Alfred, Albert, Louise, Victor Stanley and Helena Beatrice. But different ages have different role models. In 1938 the registrar for Tottenham found that at least one in five families in his area called their children after film stars, and gave Gary and Shirley as the favourites. This trend was identified by John Stroud in his novel *The Shorn Lamb* (1960), in which the three eldest children of the problem Crump family are called Rudolph (Valentino), Bebe (Daniels) and Gloria (Swanson). The practice continues, for example with names such as Tracy and Hayley (both originally surnames), though children today are perhaps more likely to be called after a favourite character in a soap opera, for instance Krystle in *Dynasty*.

In every age there are some people who attract attention by their startling choice of names for their children. One such was Charles Dickens, who seems to have viewed the christenings of his numerous offspring chiefly as an opportunity to pay tribute to those he loved and admired. He named his first son Charles Culliford Boz Dickens, and the second Walter Savage Landor. When his fourth child was baptized at St Marylebone Church, Robert Browning wrote with some amusement to Elizabeth Barrett that 'the *novus homo* glories in the praenomina Alfred d'Orsay Tennyson Dickens' (after the two godfathers). One wit was moved to verse by the occasion:

> What eye but glistens
> And what ear but listens
> When the clergy christens
> A babe of Boz.

But Edward Fitzgerald was much less charitable when he commented: 'It is one thing to worship heroes and another to lick their spittle.'

The desire to honour poets can take strange turns. Earlier this century a father brought his baby daughter to be baptized, wishing her to be called Shelley. Upon the priest's querying this name (much more unusual then than now), he explained that his wife had always been passionately fond of the *Ode to a Nightingale*, and had determined to call her child after its author. The priest protested that the poem in question had been written not by Shelley but by Keats; whereupon the father, though momentarily disconcerted, said, well, it was too late now, he was certainly not going to call his daughter Keats, she would have to be Shelley all the same. And Shelley she was duly christened.

During the eighteenth century the practice of giving children several names was firmly established. The *Oxford Dictionary of Christian Names* cites as the most extreme example of this the Wiltshire tailor who in 1781 named his son Charles Caractacus Ostorius Maximilian Gustavus Adolphus. Grandiose as this string of names is, it has been completely put in the shade in our own time by the Nelsons of Chesterfield who, on 20 April 1986, had their baby daughter baptized under no less than 140 names.* Although the vicar was happy enough to perform the ceremony, the registrar objected on the grounds that there was not enough room for the whole list either in his book or on the birth certificate.

Foundlings had of course no parents or relatives to give them a name, and one of the first duties of the parish authorities was to think of one for them. Often a name was suggested by the time or place of discovery, as Crabbe describes in *The Parish Register*:

---

* Tracy Mariclaire Lisa Tammey Samantha Christine Alexandra Candy Bonnie Ursala Zoe Nichola Patricia Lynda Kate Jean Sandra Karren Julie Jane Elizabeth Felicity Gabriella Jackie Corina Constance Arabella Clara Honor Geraldine Marylyn Fiona Erika Fillippa Anabel Elsie Amanda Cheryl Alanna Louisa Angie Beth Crystal Dawn Debbie Eileen Grace Susan Rebecca Valerie Kay Lena Margaret Anna Amy Carol Bella Avril Ava Audry Andrea Daphne Donna Cynthia Cassie Christabel Vivien Wendy Moria Jennifer Abbie Adelaide Carrissa Carla Anne Astrid Barbara Charissa Catalina Bunny Dee Hazel Iris Anthea Clarinda Bernadette Cara Alison Carrie Angela Beryl Caroline Emma Dana Vanessa Zara Violet Lynn Maggie Pamela Rosemary Ruth Cathlene Alexandrina Annette Hilary Diana Angelina Carrinna Victoria Sara Mandy Annabella Beverley Bridget Cecilia Catherine Brenda Jessica Isabella Delilah Camila Candace Helen Connie Charmaine Dorothy Melinda Nancy Mariam Vicki Selina Miriam Norma Pauline Toni Penny Shari Zsa-Zsa Queenie. She is known as Tracy.

Then by what name th'unwelcome guest to call
Was long a question, and it posed them all;
For he who lent it to a babe unknown,
Censorious men might take it for his own:
They look'd about, they gravely spoke to all,
And not one 'Richard' answered to the call.
Next they inquired the day, when, passing by,
Th'unlucky peasant heard the stranger's cry:
This known, – how food and raiment they might give,
Was next debated – for the rogue would live;
At last, with all their words and works content,
Back to their homes the prudent vestry went,
And 'Richard Monday' to the workhouse sent.

Dickens's Mr Bumble did not take nearly so much trouble. On being asked how Oliver Twist came by his name:

The beadle drew himself up with great pride, and said, 'I inwented it.'
'You, Mr. Bumble!'
'I, Mrs. Mann. We name our foundlings on alphabetical order. The last was a S – Swubble, I named him. This was T – Twist, I named *him*. The next one as comes will be Unwin, and the next Vilkins. I have got names ready-made to the end of the alphabet, and all the way through it again, when we come to Z.'
'Why, you're quite a literary character, sir!' said Mrs. Mann.
'Well, well,' said the beadle, evidently gratified with the compliment; 'perhaps I may be. Perhaps I may be, Mrs. Mann.'

Other poor foundlings were named by the minister who performed the baptism. Some might be sympathetic, like the priest at Wolstanton in Staffordshire, who entered in his register for 12 June 1698: *Baptized Providence, an infant whom her father and mother abandoned; but GOD will take care of her.* But others were less charitable, and projected their own feelings of outraged virtue on to the hapless infants in their care with such tragic names as Lament, Frendelesse, Flie-Fornication or Misericordia-Adulterina. Thomas Hardy was drawing on this tradition when he pulled out all the emotional stops in his account of Tess's baptism of her dying baby:

> The little ones kneeling round, their sleepy eyes blinking and red, awaited her preparations full of a suspended wonder which their physical heaviness at that hour would not allow to become active.
>
> The most impressed of them said:
>
> 'Be you really going to christen him, Tess?'
>
> The girl-mother replied in a grave affirmative.
>
> 'What's his name going to be?'
>
> She had not thought of that, but a name suggested by a phrase in the book of Genesis came into her head as she proceeded with the baptismal service, and now she pronounced it:
>
> 'SORROW, I baptize thee in the name of the Father, and of the Son, and of the Holy Ghost.'

A comical Australian ballad by the celebrated 'Banjo' Paterson, entitled *A Bush Christening*, hinges on the fact that the parents have forgotten to stipulate a name for their offspring:

> On the outer Barcoo where the churches are few,
> And men of religion are scanty,
> On a road never cross'd 'cept by folk that are lost
> One Michael Magee had a shanty.
>
> Now this Mike was the dad of a ten-year-old lad,
> Plump, healthy, and stoutly conditioned;
> He was strong as the best, but poor Mike had no rest
> For the youngster had never been christened.
>
> And his wife used to cry, 'If the darlin' should die
> Saint Peter would not recognize him.'
> But by luck he survived till a preacher arrived,
> Who agreed straightaway to baptize him.
>
> Now the artful young rogue, while they held their collogue,
> With his ear to the keyhole was listenin';
> And he muttered in fright, while his features turned white,
> 'What the divil and all is this christenin'?'

He was none of your dolts – he had seen them brand colts,
And it seemed to his small understanding,
If the man in the frock made him one of the flock,
It must mean something very like branding.

So away with a rush he set off for the bush,
While the tears in his eyelids they glistened –
''Tis outrageous', says he, 'to brand youngsters like me;
I'll be dashed if I'll stop to be christened!'

Like a young native dog he ran into a log,
And his father with language uncivil,
Never heeding the 'praste', cried aloud in his haste
'Come out and be christened, you divil!'

But he lay there as snug as a bug in a rug,
And his parents in vain might reprove him,
Till His Reverence spoke (he was fond of a joke)
'I've a notion', says he, 'that'll move him.

'Poke a stick up the log, give the spalpeen a prog;
Poke him aisy – don't hurt him or maim him;
'Tis not long that he'll stand, I've the water at hand,
As he rushes out this end I'll name him.

'Here he comes, and for shame! ye've forgotten the name –
Is it Patsy or Michael or Dinnis?'
Here the youngster ran out, and the priest gave a shout –
'Take your chance, anyhow, wid "Maginnis"!'

As the howling young cub ran away to the scrub
Where he knew that pursuit would be risky,
The priest, as he fled, flung a flask at his head
That was labelled 'Maginnis's Whisky'!

And Maginnis Magee has been made a J.P.,
And the one thing he hates more than sin is
To be asked by the folk, who have heard of the joke,
How he came to be christened Maginnis!

4

GIFTS

Once upon a time there lived a king and queen who were in despair because they had no children. At last, in answer to their prayers, they had a little daughter. They were overjoyed, and they invited seven fairies to the christening so that the lovely child might be blessed with many wonderful gifts.

After the ceremony a splendid feast had been arranged. Everyone was taking their place at the table when suddenly an aged fairy hobbled in. She had not been invited to the celebration because the king and queen believed her to be dead. At once they set a place for her, but the crone, convinced that she had been slighted on purpose, began to mutter under her breath. One of the younger fairies overheard her and, fearing that she might work some mischief against the little princess, hid herself so that she could be the last to speak and thus put matters right again.

After the feast the fairies, one by one, leant over the baby's cradle. The first gave her beauty, the second wisdom, the third a sweet nature, the fourth, the gift of laughter, and the fifth, a voice like a nightingale's.

The old fairy then came forward and pronounced that when the princess was fifteen she would prick her finger on a spindle and die.

Everybody shuddered at these dreadful words, at which moment the young fairy stepped out from behind a curtain and said, 'Do not be alarmed, for your daughter will not die. Instead, she will fall asleep for a hundred years and then a prince will come and wake her with a kiss.'

Traditional

In the belief of folklore, a new-born child should be presented with some salt, an egg and a coin. The salt grants protection against evil influences, and dates back to the pagan Roman custom of placing a few grains of salt on the lips of an infant on the eighth day after its birth to chase away the demons, the egg represents fertility and the coin ensures a wealthy future for the recipient. The custom of giving coins to babies is still prevalent in many areas. At the christening of the author's own baby (in 1986), an elderly woman from Yorkshire pressed a £1 coin into his hand, saying, 'It should rightly be a silver threepenny bit, but there. May you never want.' Some of the earliest christening presents on record are sums of money, and the very old, and still lively, tradition of giving silver objects on these occasions may well stem from the belief that it is lucky to do so. In Elizabeth of York's Privy Purse Expenses there is an entry for 3 July 1502: *Itm̄ the same day delivered to my Lady Bray for money by hure geven at the cristenyng of John Belles childe at Winsore by the Quenes commaundement . . . xxvjs. viijd.* Towards the end of the seventeenth century the Earl of Bedford gave a standard (and extremely handsome) present of 9 guineas to his grandchildren and his friends' children when they were christened, though one favoured grandson received 16 guineas. In our own century money is still a welcome gift in view of the innumerable things a baby needs, but it is more likely to be in the form of a cheque.

Gold and silver plate were also popular gifts, and feature in the Earl of Bedford's accounts. John Evelyn was given at his christening 'two handsom pieces of very curiously wrought, & gilt plate'. When he stood godfather to his brother George's daughter Mary in 1648 he clearly felt that he had done extremely well by her, for he described his present in great detail in his diary: in the normal way he does not mention such things.

I presented my *Niepce* a piece of *Plate* which cost me 18 pounds and caus'd this Inscription to be set on it

In Memoriam facti
Anno CIↃ.IↃC.XLIIX Cal. Decemb: Vlll. Virginum castiss.
Xtianorum Innocentiss: Nept: Suaviss: Mariae Johann: Evelynus
Avunculus (et) Susceptor Vasculum hoc cum Epigraphe
L.M.Q.D.
Ave Maria Gratia sis plena, Dominus tecum.

Silver spoons, especially Apostle spoons, so called because their stems end in figures of the Apostles, were frequently given. Wealthy godparents might give their godchildren a whole set of twelve, while the less well-to-do would be content with one. Obviously this was a particularly appropriate gift if the child was being named after one of the Apostles. In 1558 'a spoyne, the gyft of Master Fletcher, all gylt wyth the pycture of Saynte Matthewe' was presented to young Matthewe Quarle 'ate hys chrisome'. Ordinary spoons were given too. In Jersey it was traditional to give a boy a silver soup spoon, while girls received half a dozen teaspoons, all made by local silversmiths. On 26 May 1661, Samuel Pepys 'heard how Mrs. Browne, Sir W. Batten's sister, is brought to bed, and I to be one of the godfathers, which I could not nor did deny. Which, however, did trouble me very much to be at charge to no purpose, so that I could not sleep hardly all night, but in the morning I bethought myself, and I think it is very well I should do it'. Two days later he went shopping for a present in Cheapside, and on the 29th 'rose early and having made myself fine, and put six spoons and a porringer of silver in my pocket to give away to-day, Sir W. Pen and I took coach'. The day was a disappointment, however, for as noted earlier the baby was not given the name Samuel, and Pepys took his present home again in a huff. He did not finally hand over the spoons until 1 August, and even then he was still nursing his grievance, for poor little John Browne never received the porringer. But presents might be deferred even where offence had not been taken: Pepys's wife was godmother at a christening on 21 December of the same year, and it was not until 10 January that she gave the mother a cup and spoon for her godchild.

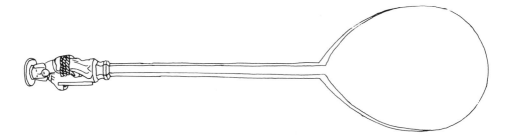

Silver Apostle spoon, late seventeenth century, London

Silver sugar basin and sifter, 1907

Silver egg cup and spoon, *c.* 1900

Later on it became customary to add a fork and a knife or napkin-ring to the spoon. In 1900 Richard, the son of Robert and Mary Hamilton, received from his father's colonel and fellow officers a silver mug, napkin-ring, spoon and fork. The last three items could well have been purchased from the Army & Navy Stores: a set in chased silver, complete with a case, cost 30*s.* 6*d.* in 1902.

In 1663 Betty Adams wrote to thank her brother, Sir Ralph Verney, who was godfather to her son, for his present of 'a silver sugar box & coddel [caudle] cup'. (This, together with the inclusion of a sugar basin and sifter in the christening presents section of *The Army & Navy Stores Catalogue* for 1907, would seem to prove that it is not only modern babies who are addicted to sugar.) Silver cups, mugs and bowls were very widely given. In 1638 Joyce Jeffries of Herefordshire paid £5. 5s. 6d. for a silver tankard for her goddaughter Joyce Walsh, and four years later she gave a Hereford goldsmith 'for a silver christening bowle to little Joyce Lawrence at 5 shillings and 8 pence an ounze, 48 shillings 10 pence'. Dickens's misanthropic Dumps, unable to evade his duties, 'purchased a handsome silver mug for the infant Kitterbell, upon which he ordered the initials "F.C.W.K.", with the customary untrained grape-vine-looking flourishes, and a large full stop, to be engraved forthwith'. But alas, the mug was not to reach its destination, for

> . . . as he was crossing the corner of Hatton Garden, a man, apparently intoxicated, rushed against him, and would have knocked him down, had he not been providentially caught by a very genteel young man, who happened to be close to him at the time. The shock so disarranged Dumps's nerves, as well as his dress, that he could hardly stand. The gentleman took his arm, and in the kindest manner walked with him as far as Furnival's Inn. Dumps, for about the first time in his life, felt grateful and polite; and he and the gentlemanly-looking young man parted with mutual expressions of goodwill.

But gentlemanly appearances can be deceiving, and when Dumps reached his nephew's house the mug was no longer in his pocket.

Christening mugs were not necessarily silver. In her *Crafts, Customs and Legends of Wales* Mary Corbett Harris describes two inscribed china mugs, of a rich pink colour with touches of gold, which were made to commemorate christenings. And in the Salisbury and South Wiltshire Museum there is a magnificent four-handled bowl and cover dating from 1692. It is made of Wiltshire brownware, decorated with stylized patterns, and with a crude inscription round the rim: *Here is the gest of the barly korne Glad Ham I the Cild is Born RK SK.*

When John Forster was godfather to one of Dickens's children, Douglas Jerrold quipped, 'I hope that if you gave the child a mug it was *not* your own.'

Other presents included egg-cups (perhaps the last lingering trace of the custom of giving a baby an egg), pencils and teething-rings. Thackeray's William Dobbin, godfather to the child of his beloved Amelia Osborne, 'exerted his ingenuity in the purchase of cups, spoons, papboats, and corals for this little Christian'. Coral was credited with many properties which made it a suitable present. It was held to protect against witchcraft and to ward off the evil eye; it was said to grow pale when the child was unwell; and it was thought to cure wind. On a more practical level, it was a good material for babies to cut their teeth on. When the baby Augustus Hare's parents enthusiastically handed him over to his godmother for adoption, in 1834, they sent with him only

Francis Thynne, after Hans Eworth (*c.* 1520–74)

two little nightshirts and a coral necklace. Elizabethan portraits show children holding magnificent sets of coral. The infant Robert Delisle appears in a family group by Gheeraerts clutching one which appears to be attached to his dress by a red ribbon. Francis Thynne was painted by Hans Eworth in 1564, at the age of six months. He is shown standing upright, with remarkable precocity, holding a very ornate coral. It is of the white variety, in the shape of a curved cone about half the length of his hand, mounted on a slender stick. Three silver bells are suspended from the handle, and the whole thing is attached to his waist by a double silver chain. Nearly three hundred years later Cecilia Ridley described a very similar object when she wrote to her mother, in 1842: 'Lady Ridley has sent Baby a beautiful coral set in engraved gold with two little gold bells and the crest engraved on it. It is really a beautiful thing and Baby has it hung round his waist and plays with it.' Even in the 1950s it was still popular, and 'Miss Read' noted in her *Village Diary*: '[Malcolm Annett's] christening is fixed for the first Sunday in October and I am looking forward to a trip into Caxley to find a really attractive silver rattle and coral, worthy of such a fine boy.'

The Puritans, hating the association of a religious ceremony with such superstitious ideas, tried to put an end to the giving of coral. For them, the only suitable present was a Bible. And indeed the obvious appropriateness of this, particularly with more widespread literacy, meant that Bibles remained fashionable presents up to and throughout the nineteenth century, especially if they were prettily bound and fitted with silver clasps. They are still widely given today, wherever parents and godparents are practising Christians. But such an uncompromisingly edifying gift was scorned in worldly circles, as the fictional Geraldine Vernon recounts in *The Ladies' Treasury* of the mid-1860s:

I remember Mrs. Brown said, when Bertha was expecting an addition to her family, that she hoped she should choose her child's godfathers and godmothers more wisely than she had herself done. She remarked that she had asked a very wealthy old goldsmith, Mr. Nugget, to be godfather to Bertha, hoping he would give her child a gold mug, and a fork and spoon in the same precious metal. He accepted the office, came to the christening, stayed a week, never made any present at all, and never took any notice of his godchild from that day to the day of his death (about a year ago), when in his will he left her his family Bible, 'The whole duty of Man', and a rare old Latin edition of 'The Fathers'. This bequest, which some would, and all ought to, prize, only excited the anger and disdain of Mrs. Brown and Bertha Thornton.

In his continuation of Stow's *Annals*, Howe describes another kind of gift, traditional in Elizabethan times.

At that time and indeed for many years before, it was the custom for godfathers and godmothers to give, at the baptism of children, christning shirts, with little bands and cuffs wrought with silk or blue thread: the best of them, for chief personages, were edged with a small lace of black silk and gold, the highest price of which, for great men's children, as seldom above a noble; and of the common sort, two, three, four, or five shillings a-piece.

He adds that by his own time, that is the mid-seventeenth century, people gave cups and spoons instead. Sometimes the shirts were accompanied by mittens. Alice Morse Earle, in her study of American colonial costume, has described such a set. It was made for William Bradford, one of the Pilgrim Fathers and second Governor of the Plymouth Colony, who was born in 1590. 'All are of firm, close-woven, homespun linen, but the little mittens have been worn at the ends by the active friction of baby hands, and are patched with red and yellow figured "chiney" or calico. This may have been part of their ornamentation when first made, but it looks extraneous. The sleeves of this shirt are plaited or goffered in a way that seems wholly lost.'

A later idea was a 'christening glass'. When a couple got married they were presented with a jug; as each child was born a matching glass, inscribed with its initials and date of birth, was added to the set.

In poorer households presents were more functional, often taking the form of money or a contribution to the christening party. In France in the nineteenth century it seems to have been customary for the godmother to provide the child's outfit. In Zola's *La Terre* Mme Charles produces a dress and bonnet for her goddaughter Laure, though in the event it arrives too late for the ceremony. She also brings six boxes of sweets for the mother and one for the priest. At the christening of little Nana, in the same author's *L'Assommoir*, we are told that 'on Saturday evening, Mme Lorilleux brought the presents for her goddaughter: a bonnet that had cost 35 *sous* and a christening robe, pleated and trimmed with narrow lace, which she had got for six francs on account of its being shop-soiled'.

One of the most popular presents, from the mid-seventeenth century to the mid-nineteenth century, was a commemorative pincushion. These highly decorative objects were in fact extremely functional, the valuable part of the gift being the pins themselves, and the cushion being an elaborate form of gift-wrapping. Pins during this period were made of brass, and the heads, which consisted of a small piece of coiled wire, were put on separately, a job that was entrusted to young children. As it took more than twenty people to make a pin from start to finish, they were expensive items, and the term 'pin-money' connoted a substantial sum. They were also indispensable. Safety pins were not invented until 1878, and until then babies' clothes were held together with numbers of ordinary, straight pins. Accidents must have been quite common, and Kitterbell's note to his uncle Dumps on this subject was not just a humorous fancy of Dickens's: 'I open this note to say that we have just discovered the cause of little Frederick's restlessness. It is not fever, as I apprehended, but a small pin, which nurse accidentally stuck in his leg yesterday evening. We have taken it out, and he appears more composed, though he still sobs a good deal.' (When modern babies cry for no discernible reason, their mothers are still advised to check whether there is a pin sticking into them, the likelihood of which is so remote that the advice must surely be prompted by a lingering folk memory.) Rather than presenting the mother of a new baby with a simple packet of pins, welcome though this would be, it was the custom to make a cushion for them, usually of white satin, and to stick the pins into it in a decorative pattern, spelling out a sentence or verse in the middle. The most common were 'Welcome Sweet Babe' or 'Welcome Little Stranger', but more ambitious examples survive, such as 'May Health Protect the Smiling Babe and Happiness the Mother' or even 'Hail to this teeming stage of strife, Hail lovely miniature of life'. There would be hearts and flowers all around and a border, sometimes of lace, sometimes formed of extra long pins stuck porcupine-fashion into the

Early nineteenth-century pincushions

edges of the cushion. There was a good reason for presenting the pincushion at the christening rather than before the birth. In their book *Costume for Births, Marriages and Deaths*, Cunnington and Lucas noted a belief still prevalent in the nineteenth century in the Isle of Wight that pins stuck into a cushion were related to pain in childbirth – 'More pins, more pain' – with the result that midwives insisted that all pins be removed at the onset of labour (just as all knots in the mother's clothing were loosened). The donor who thought to present her gift in good time, would therefore see all her meticulous work undone. From the mid-nineteenth century solid-headed pins began to appear at a reasonable price, so although pincushions were still everyday items, they ceased to be fashionable christening gifts.

In Warwickshire present-giving was not limited to the christening day. There it was traditional for godparents to present their godchildren with a 'Coventry godcake' every New Year's Day. This was a triangular cake of flaky pastry filled with mincemeat, measuring anything up to 18 inches per side, glazed with beaten egg-white and sugar and with three slits cut in the top to represent the Trinity. (For the old recipe, see Appendix 3, pp. 160-1.)

Nowadays, with smaller houses and a rushed pace of life, there is a trend away from elaborate but useless christening presents which either demand tedious cleaning or stay in the cupboard growing tarnished. Godparents prefer to give a useful and decorative item for the nursery, such as a set of tableware, a brightly painted little chair with the child's name on it, or perhaps a commemorative sampler; or they opt for something that the child will enjoy in years to come – antiques of all kinds, especially framed prints, jewellery, or even wine. The gifts given to the present writer's baby typify this trend: a Royal Worcester mug, bowl and plate with a Noah's Ark pattern; an illuminated Gospels; and an antique, leather-bound edition of *The Pilgrim's Progress. Debrett's* suggests in addition that an 'old country custom' which might well be revived is that of planting a tree to commemorate a christening.

Traditionally it was not only the baby who received presents at the christening. Practically everybody who had had a part in the birth or the ceremony expected to be remembered on this day, and christenings could be very expensive for both parents and guests.

In theory the sacrament of baptism was freely administered. Bishop Grandisson decreed in 1355 'that no priest could deny, or presume to deny, any Sacrament to his parishioners by demanding money, but that he might afterwards take what the people chose to offer him'. In practice this voluntary offering often consisted of an invitation to dinner after the service, but it was sometimes much more generous. Parson Woodforde, who took genuine pleasure in the discharge of his duties, was the more delighted when, after he had baptized Hambleton Thomas Custance, 'Mr. Custance immediately after the ceremony came to me and desired me to accept a small Present; it was wrapped up in a Piece of white Paper very neat, and on opening of it, I found it contained nothing less than the sum of 4.4.0.' The following year he baptized another Custance baby;

this time the father presented him with 'a Norwich Bank Note of five Guineas, wrapped up in some Writing Paper', as well as an invitation to dinner. This was typical of eighteenth-century country life, where squire and parson were on easy social terms. In Victorian London things were very much more formal and impersonal, and etiquette books suggest that fees of a guinea upwards were not unknown. Paul Dombey's father (who admittedly would have been stiff and proud whatever the time and place) 'informed the clergyman how much pleasure it would have given him to have solicited the honour of his company at dinner, but for the unfortunate state of his household affairs' (his wife having died in childbirth). He then, we are told, paid the fees. By 1872 the practice of charging for baptism had become unacceptably widespread, and it was forbidden by an act passed on 18 July of that year; but, as an Edwardian etiquette book explained, 'it is not unusual for those who can afford it, and wish to show a kindly feeling, to make the clergyman a present, which may range from one guinea to perhaps ten'. There were other tips to be distributed after the service: Woodforde's clerk received 10s. 6d. from Squire Custance; at Paul Dombey's christening the family party did not make their escape until 'the pew-opener (whose cough was very bad again) had been remembered, and the beadle gratified, and the sexton (who was accidentally on the door-steps, looking with great interest at the weather) not forgotten'; and Edwardian parents were warned that 'there will be various underlings at the church who will be on the outlook for a fee, but it is usually sufficient if the father recognises the services of the verger, or whoever it may be that opens the church and has everything in readiness'.

When the christening party returned home from church, the midwife, nurse and servants were all waiting to be rewarded by both parents and godparents. Henry Verney, standing in for his brother Ralph at a family christening in 1655, wrote: 'I have given 20s. to the nurse and 20s. to the midwife and 10s. to the nurse-keeper as you ordered.' A few years later Pepys noted in his diary that on one occasion he parted with 10s. to the midwife, 5s. to the nurse and 2s. to the maid of the house; on another he grumbled that 'it cost me 20s. between the midwife and the two nurses to-day'. At the christening of Parson Woodforde's niece, he recorded that 'being Godfather I gave to the Midwife 0.5.0., to the Nurse gave 0.5.0. To four servants – 1/0 each – gave 0.4.0.'. After the Custance

christening, doubtless still glowing from his own gift of 5 guineas and an
excellent dinner, he gave George the servant half a crown. His
contemporary Thomas Turner was much less munificent: he gave
between sixpence and a shilling to the maid of the house, and even at the
grandest christening he attended he gave the nurse only 2*s.*, while at the
humblest she received only sixpence. By the middle of the next
century a 'trifling present to the nurse' was still the expected thing, and
this custom persisted at least until the 1920s, and probably for as long as
it was the norm to employ a private nurse at all. An Edwardian writer
observed drily that 'relatives are supposed to be so overjoyed at the event
that they give the nurse anything from five shillings to five pounds; but
under ordinary circumstances, in ordinary homes, she is doubtless well
pleased with half-a-crown'.

Not all nurses received their presents in cash. Dickens gives us a
pathetic example of a thoroughly unwelcome gift:

> Mr. Dombey, in the meanwhile, had issued orders for the attendance
> of Richards, who now entered curtseying, but without the baby; Paul
> being asleep after the fatigues of the morning. Mr. Dombey, having
> delivered a glass of wine to this vassal, addressed her in the following
> words . . .
>
> 'During the six months or so, Richards, which have seen you an
> inmate of this house, you have done your duty. Desiring to connect
> some little service to you with this occasion, I considered how I could
> best effect that object. . . . Having the power of nominating a child on
> the foundation of an ancient establishment, called (from a worshipful
> company) the Charitable Grinders; where not only is a wholesome
> education bestowed upon the scholars, but where a dress and badge is
> likewise provided for them; I have (first communicating, through
> Mrs. Chick, with your family) nominated your eldest son to an
> existing vacancy; and he has this day, I am informed, assumed the
> habit. The number of her son, I believe,' said Mr. Dombey, turning to
> his sister and speaking of the child as if he were a hackney-coach, 'is
> one hundred and forty-seven. Louisa, you can tell her.'
>
> 'One hundred and forty-seven,' said Mrs. Chick. 'The dress,
> Richards, is a nice, warm, blue baize tailed coat and cap, turned up
> with orange-coloured binding; red worsted stockings; and very strong

leather small-clothes. One might wear the articles one's self,' said Mrs. Chick, with enthusiasm, 'and be grateful.'

'There, Richards!' said Miss Tox. 'Now indeed, you *may* be proud. The Charitable Grinders!'

'I am sure I am very much obliged, sir,' returned Richards faintly, 'and take it very kind that you should remember my little ones.' At the same time a vision of Biler as a Charitable Grinder, with his very small legs encased in the serviceable clothing described by Mrs. Chick, swam before Richards's eyes, and made them water.

'I am very glad to see you have so much feeling, Richards,' said Miss Tox.

'It makes one almost hope, it really does,' said Mrs. Chick, who prided herself on taking trustful views of human nature, 'that there may yet be some faint spark of gratitude and right feeling in the world.'

Richards deferred to these compliments by curtseying and murmuring her thanks; but finding it quite impossible to recover her spirits from the disorder into which they had been thrown by the image of her son in his precocious nether garments, she gradually approached the door and was heartily relieved to escape by it.

From *Harper's Bazaar*, 1880

5

CLOTHES

Its eyes are blue and bright,
Its cheeks like rose;
Its simple robes unite
Whitest of calicoes
With lawn, and satin bows.

Thomas Hardy, *The Christening*

A white garment has always been an important feature of the baptismal ceremony, symbolizing the new and guiltless life into which the candidate has been reborn. In England such a garment has traditionally been known as a chrisom, or chrisom cloth. Originally it was a cloth that was put over the child's head after the anointing, and served to prevent the chrism, or holy oil, from being rubbed off. Later this function was fulfilled by a cap, and the chrisom became a robe that was put on to the child after the immersion but before the anointing. In the Prayer Book of Edward VI (1549), the minister is directed to dress the baby in the robe with these words: 'Take this white vesture for a token of the innocencie, whiche by Gods grace in this holy sacramente of Baptisme, is given unto thee.' The child then wore the chrisom for three or four weeks, until its mother came to be churched. Tiny babies were sometimes known as 'chrisom children' for this reason: in *Henry V* Mistress Pistol describes how Falstaff, on his deathbed, 'went away an it had been any christom child', in other words as peacefully as a baby. When the mother was churched, the Prayer Book ordained that 'the Crisomes be brought to the churche, and delyvered to the priestes after the accustomed maner'; they were then used in ablutions. If, however, the child died within a month of its baptism, the chrisom served as its shroud. These customs have all died away. Nowadays, if a white gown is used at all, the baby generally arrives at church already wearing it. As recently as 1946, however, W.E. Tate noted in *The Parish Chest* that in some places it was still customary for the godmother to cover the baby's face with a white cambric handkerchief immediately after the actual baptism.

Although christenings are primarily religious functions, they were also, at least until the beginning of the twentieth century, the occasion when the baby made its first public appearance, and mothers were naturally anxious that it should look its best. Up to and including the eighteenth century, babies were carried to church for baptism in a richly coloured and textured wrap. This went by a variety of names. Most commonly it was called a bearing cloth, but it was also known as a christening sheet or a cade cloth. In Dorset it was a palm or pall, in Devon a pane or pame. It was very large – approximately five feet long and slightly less wide – and often so heavy, particularly at grand christenings, that the four corners had to be supported. In 1663 Pepys recorded that Lady Jemimah Crew was 'one of the four ladies that hold up the mantle at the christening this afternoon of the Duke's child'. After the ceremony the baby stayed wrapped up to be admired at the celebration. Being thus designed for display, bearing cloths were as gorgeous as possible. Red was a favourite colour – in *Henry VI* the Duke of Gloucester warns the Bishop of Winchester:

> Thy scarlet robes, as a child's bearing-cloth,
> I'll use to carry thee out of this place . . .

Clearly the image was suggested to the Duke by the similarity in colour. The fabric was usually silk, satin or velvet, elaborately trimmed with lace, fringe or embroidery. We have descriptions of some of these cloths. The author of *Dorsetshire Folk-lore*, writing at the end of the nineteenth century, possessed one made of rich crimson satin, lined with pink silk and with a double edging of silver lace all round; and he described another of rich stiff silk lined with white satin. Alice Morse Earle, in her study of American colonial costume, examined and recorded several. In 1590 William Bradford of the Plymouth Colony had one made of rich crimson silk scattered with pink and yellow flowers worked in tiny silk cross-stitches at 6-inch intervals. Another was of yellow satin decorated

The Saltonstall Family, *c.* 1636/7, by David des Granges (1611/13–75?). The infant is swaddled, and wrapped in a scarlet bearing cloth edged with gilt lace.

with white floss. Many were embroidered with initials, emblems, texts and phrases such as 'God Bless the Babe'. A particularly splendid one was worked with a picture showing a child pointing to the Tree of Knowledge, which bore not fruit but books: the *New England Primer*, Janeways's *Holy Children*, and so forth. Occasionally they came in pairs. She quotes an inventory of the seventeenth century which includes a cloth of white satin embroidered with yellow silk, 44 inches by 34, and another of yellow silk lined with white satin, 54 inches by 48. She suggests that the child would have been placed on the larger cloth and covered by the smaller. In 1666 Mun (Edmund) Verney's wife Mary (the son and daughter-in-law of Sir Ralph and Lady Verney) prepared two 'fine white mantles' of different sizes for her baby Ralph, which may have been used in this way, though the text informs us that the larger one was to lay over the head of the cradle and the smaller to wrap the baby in, either as it lay in bed or when it was taken out.

In addition to being wrapped in a bearing cloth, the baby might be carried to church on a cushion, on which it could be laid down when the time came to undress it. Like the cloths, these cushions were very elaborate. A magnificent example dated 1644 is preserved at Parham Park in Sussex. Measuring 14 inches by 11, it is worked in very fine tent stitch on canvas, and depicts the finding of Moses in the bulrushes. Pharaoh's daughter kneels by the baby in his basket, with a handmaiden on either side, all three having double eyebrows to show how surprised they are; while the sun, moon and stars shine down on a landscape that includes a leopard, a grasshopper and a kingfisher. The

Embroidered christening cushion, 1644, 'The Finding of Moses'

whole cushion has an elaborate lace border that incorporates strips of parchment edged with silk, folded into zigzags.

Of course the child's christening outfit consisted of more than just the bearing cloth. Alice Morse Earle lists one from the seventeenth century that comprised the pair of cloths mentioned earlier, and in addition a tight-fitting, lined cap of white figured satin, to be worn underneath a second cap of white satin embroidered with sprays of gold silk, a pair of lace-trimmed linen mittens with yellow silk embroidery on the backs of the fingers, and a pair of deep, white satin cuffs, embroidered and trimmed with lace, which were worn by the adult – presumably the godmother – who carried the baby. Parts of another seventeenth-century christening set are preserved in the Castle Museum, Nottingham. These comprise a long bib with a separate collar, a headpiece that fastens under the chin, a stayband, a piece to tie over the lower half of the body, and a two-layered piece thought to be a pincushion cover. All are made of linen, embroidered with laid linen cord. In both these lists the robe is conspicuous by its absence. This may be because its place was supplied by the chrisom, or because the baby would have been swaddled – a practice that prevailed well into the eighteenth century and would have made a robe unnecessary. In her study of the list of 'Child bed Linning' compiled by Mary East in 1698, Pamela Clabburn has suggested that two of the entries may refer to a christening outfit. These are '1 Rich white Sattain Mantle lind wth Sasnet [a thin silk fabric] with Cape & Sleeves of ye Same' and '1 fine point [i.e. lace] Sute of Bib Cuffs gloves two pinners [caps] & double point forehead Cloth'. Again there is no mention of a robe, but the author argues that at this time the word 'mantle' was used to mean either a bearing cloth or a sleeved coat or gown. All the above garments are white, and if we are to believe the Countess of Derby, Charlotte de la Tremoille, this was not typical. In 1628 she wrote: 'I have informed Madam of the baptism of your nephew. . . . I had him dressed in white after the French fashion, for here [i.e. in England] they dress them in colours, which I do not like.'

Grown-ups enjoyed dressing themselves up for christenings too. Pepys and his wife both put on fine clothes for such occasions. When the latter attended the christening of the Pierce baby as proxy godmother in 1660, she took special pains with her appearance, for her husband remarked that 'this the first day that ever I saw my wife wear black patches since we were married'. (This was a fashion for applying small spots of black silk or velvet to the face, which supposedly set off a good complexion.) But on another occasion there was an argument: 'So to dinner, and then had a little scolding with my wife for not being fine enough to go to the christening to-day, which she excused by being ill, as she was indeed, and cried, but I was in an ill humour and ashamed, indeed, that she should not go dressed.' For the christening of her little son Ralph, in 1666, Mary Verney wore a waistcoat and mantle of white satin, a white summer gown lined with white silk and a white mohair petticoat.

During the course of the eighteenth century, as swaddling was gradually abandoned, christening robes began to appear. Several have been preserved in museums, and although they are not the virtuoso pieces of needlework which they later became, they are none the less very beautiful. They were generally made of white or cream satin and followed the style of adult dresses in being open all the way down the front, the edges trimmed with braid or lace, revealing the petticoat beneath. The bodice had vertical pin-tucks and the whole thing was about a yard long. But the outer wrap, whether mantle or cloak, was still the most important item, a fact recognized by Mrs Gaskell when she had her heroine Sylvia plan her baby's christening at the end of the century:

> 'Hester may be godmother, and I'll ha' t'dove-coloured silk as yo' gave me afore we were married made up into a cloak for it to go to church in.'
>
> 'I got it for thee,' said Philip, a little disappointed. 'It'll be too good for the baby.'
>
> 'Eh! but I'm so careless, I should be spilling something on it? But if thou got it for me I cannot find i' my heart for t'wear it on baby, and I'll have it made for a christening gown for mysel'. But I'll never feel at my ease in it, for fear of spoiling it.'

Susan Sibbald recalled that at the christening of her sister in 1792, 'Grace had laid out for the occasion a most beautiful blue and white satin mantle; blue hat and feathers, presents from Lady Paine, one of her godmothers.' The more humbly born Baby Kitterbell made his appearance at Dickens's *Bloomsbury Christening* (1836) 'packed up in a

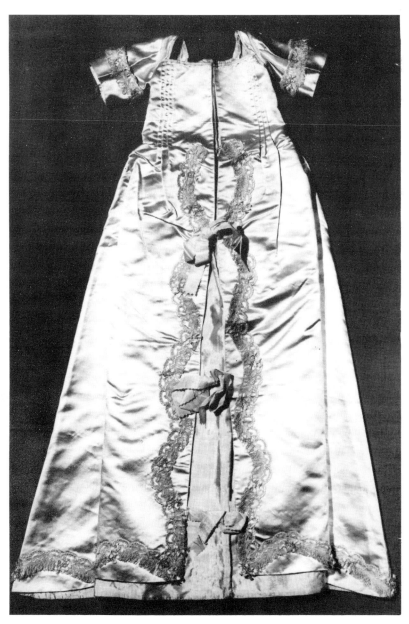

A christening robe of 1760–80; ivory satin trimmed with silk braid.

blue mantle trimmed with white fur'. Caroline Clive's sister Mary, describing the christening of their nephew in 1835, refers to the 'baby in his beautiful christening mantle', and a year later she becomes quite lyrical in her specifications for the perfect article:

> 'I cannot overcome the wish to have Georgey christened in a mantle although I have persuaded myself not to have a seven guinea one. But I mean to have a white satin one covered with India muslin and I should be very much obliged to you to get me five yards of *faultless* white satin. It must be a most luscious article, soft as down and white as snow, with a *soupçon* of a pink blush upon it – at least it must have a bloom from the richness of its constitution. All these virtues they say can be got for six or seven shillings a yard. It must be a French satin as the best English have a degree of wiriness always. In short it must be a satin that you could not help loving. It must be trimmed either with silk fringe or with swansdown. Swansdown seems to me a beau ideal but I leave it to your discretion when you see them together, and yet it sounds as if Bunting would look so *very* pretty in satin and swansdown.'

But by now the robe was establishing its supremacy. Only a few years later, in 1842, Cecilia Ridley described to her mother the christening of her eldest son, and how 'Baby was brought down in the evening, clad, for the first and last time in his life, in white satin, and looked beautiful.' The nature of the garment is clear, for she goes on to mention that 'all the maids came up to see Baby in his christening robe'. A couple of years later she wrote again:

> I have an important event to tell you, for Wee Baby was christened yesterday. . . . Baby re-entered his long clothes for the day in order to wear the beautiful robe that is kept for the occasion and which he has almost outgrown now [he was nearly six months old by that time]. It is a foolish thing, a vast of money, but very pretty of its kind. . . . Little darling, he really looks so pretty and lively and seems so well now, it is quite delightful.

In 1865 *Enquire Within Upon Everything* ruled that 'the dress of the parties attending a christening should be what may be termed demi-costume, or half-costume; but the infant should be robed in the choicest manner that the circumstances will allow'. By now this meant an elaborately embroidered robe. Its very elaboration, and hence its cost either in money or in human effort, ensured that it was kept for successive children and even handed down to later generations. Many mothers chose to make their first child's christening robe themselves, and as all Victorian women were competent seamstresses, and many were superlative, it was a delightful opportunity for them to show what they could do. Writing of baby clothes in general, *Harper's Bazaar* commented in 1893: 'For this is the chief beauty of these little garments – that they are made precious by the needle-work that is put into them. The first baby usually has a good deal of this same handiwork about his clothes, and the second generally wears out his elder brother's dainty garments, while poor little number three and his successors must depend upon the sewing machine for the stitching to their frocks.' Christening robes were rewarding to make precisely because they could be worn by number three and his successors. Their actual construction was not necessarily complicated: it was the embroidery and trimming that provided the opportunity for virtuosity. But even a mediocre needlewoman could get very pretty results by judicious use of machine-made trimmings, as a pattern recently reproduced in *The Victorian Nursery Book* suggests:

TO MAKE A CHRISTENING ROBE – take half a width of muslin and run tucks three and three with about four inches between each. Cut them apart. In paper cut the pattern of the front of the robe, which is to be a gore twenty-eight inches at the bottom, and ten inches at the top. Cut the half of it in paper, and allow three inches for the centre and outside insertion. Between every three tucks place a row of insertion, laying each on the paper pattern, so as to cut them the right length and not waste the embroidery which is expensive. Between every three tucks there must be a piece of inch wide embroidered insertion. Cut both tucks and insertion a little longer than the pattern to allow for working up, then neatly join them. Down the centre there is a row of embroidery, bordered each side by edging, and this is repeated at each side and carried round the bottom. A plain breadth of wide muslin completes the skirt, which is bordered all round by an embroidered flounce four inches deep. The

A christening robe of 1877; white cotton with embroidered panels and flounces.

body is composed of a stomacher [a wedge-shaped centre front panel] of two tucks and one insertion, placed alternately. An insertion double-edged, occupies the centre, and the braces [shoulder straps], which form a berthe [falling frill] behind, are of the flouncing embroidery that robes the front of the skirt. The sleeves are plain, but covered with a frill of the flouncing. The waist and neck-band are made of insertion, and a narrow edge finishes the top. Christening robes for babes are sometimes made of lace instead of embroidery; but of course this requires everything *en suite* in richness and costliness, and is by no means necessary. Many parents prefer to use a plain robe for the christening.

Other resolute do-it-yourselfers adapted different crafts to the purpose. In the Gallery of English Costume in Manchester there is a panel for the front of a robe made entirely of tatting, and in 1851 Sarah Ann Cunliffe knitted a complete robe, using 6,300 yards of cotton and working an incredible total of 1,464,859 stitches, though this was doubtless intended as a showpiece for the Great Exhibition rather than as a precedent for other knitters. (For a contemporary pattern, see Appendix 2, pp. 148–53.)

Not every mother had either the leisure or the desire to make her baby's robe herself. A popular, if expensive, choice was to have it made of lace, especially Honiton lace, which was chosen by Queen Victoria for the christening robe of her first child, Vicky, in 1841. (This robe has been worn by all the royal babies ever since.) But in the middle years of the century the most fashionable robes were made of so-called 'Ayrshire work'. This was a kind of very fine embroidery worked in white thread on fine, almost transparent, white muslin, consisting of raised satin stitch and French knots, cut-work and delicate needlepoint fillings. It originated at the end of the eighteenth century, when the flimsy imported Indian muslins were ousting the stiff and stately home-produced silks from the forefront of fashion. It was a speciality of Ayrshire, being carried out as a cottage industry by the wives and daughters of local miners and ironworkers, though later there was some competition from Ireland. It was poorly paid and exceedingly taxing on the eyes: some of the older workers, whose vision had been fatally impaired by years of the work, resorted to the agonizing expedient of

Christening robes from *Harrod's Catalogue*, 1895, with (*l. to r.*) all round skirt, 2 guineas; Princess front, 21*s.* 9*d.*; Princess front, trimmings of insertion and book muslin, 15*s.* 6*d.*

bathing their eyes in whisky because it caused a temporary sharpening of eyesight. Originally each piece of embroidery was carried out by the same worker from beginning to end, but as the industry became more organized the work was subdivided and each worker would be responsible for only one type of pattern or stitch.

Christening robes were generally of the cut described above, with a high waist, short sleeves and a long skirt, and the embroidery concentrated on the centre front of the bodice, and the long flared centre front skirt panel, which was also edged with a scalloped flounce; though after about 1870 the 'Princess' line was popular, following adult fashions, the front panel of bodice and skirt being cut in one piece without a waist seam. In order to show off the embroidery to the best advantage, robes at this time were immensely long. Writing in 1903, Alice Morse Earle observed that 'within a few years we have shortened the long clothes worn by youngest infants; twenty-five years ago the handsome dress of an infant, such as the christening-robe, was so long that when the child was held on the arm of its standing nurse or mother, the edge of the robe barely escaped touching the ground'. (She might have added that one of the main reasons for this change was the introduction of the perambulator, first patented in 1853 and increasing in popularity throughout the second half of the century. Early Victorian babies of any social pretensions whatever spent much of their time being carried about in a nursemaid's arms, in which position their long and lavish robes commanded suitable admiration. But on an infant sitting up in a pram, covered by blankets, such garments were wasted, and as a result they passed from fashion, to be replaced by elaborate bonnets.)

Around the turn of the century christening robes were more ornate and richly trimmed than ever. In 1895 Harrod's was selling hand-made robes trimmed with insertion and real Torchon lace at 21s. 9d. for a Princess front and 2 guineas for an all round skirt, and a cheaper model with a Princess front and trimmings of insertion and book muslin for 15s. 6d. Their infants' robes for everyday wear at this time were priced between 9s. 6d. and 16s. The *Army & Navy Stores Catalogue* for 1907 includes a particularly lavish outfit consisting of an embroidered muslin robe trimmed with insertion, with the huge puffed sleeves characteristic of that time and a great knot of ribbons hanging from the yoke seam; there is a full vandyked flounce round the bottom and the lower half of the skirt is embroidered with sprays of flowers. To wear over it there is a cloak of silk bengaline (corded silk) with a shoulder cape and a deep, falling collar, all the edges being trimmed with a generous flounce of guipure lace. The robe cost £2. 15s. and the cloak 6 guineas. The baby in the illustration reclines on a cushion, its face framed by the frilly edge of its cap, completely dwarfed by the splendour of its apparel.

These beautiful robes, whether lovingly home-made or expensively bought, were treasured and carefully handed down from one child to the next. Today they are so highly prized by the families who own them, and so eagerly sought after by those who do not, that it seems almost incredible that in the last quarter of the century the craze for modernity led to their being despised in some quarters; but so it was. In *Lark Rise to Candleford* Flora Thompson described how the vicar's daughter kept a stock of baby clothes to lend to the needy villagers:

> The little garments on loan were all good quality and nicely trimmed with embroidery and hand tucking. The clergyman's daughter also kept two christening robes to lend to the mothers, and made a new

frock, as a gift, for every baby's 'shortening'. . . . She got little credit for this. The mothers, like the children, looked upon the small garments, both loaned and given, as a provision of Nature. Indeed, they were rather inclined to criticize. One woman ripped off the deep flounce of old Buckinghamshire lace from the second-best christening robe and substituted a frill of coarse, machine-made embroidery, saying she was not going to take her child to church 'trigged out' in that old-fashioned trash. As she had not troubled to unpick the stitches, the lace was torn beyond repair, and the gown ever after was decidedly second-best, for the best one was the old Rectory family christening robe and made of the finest lawn, tucked and inserted all over with real Valenciennes.

From the same author's *Still Glides the Stream* we get a very clear picture of the clothes worn by infant and adults alike at a country christening towards the end of the century, among unpretentious, but not impoverished, folk:

[Charity] remembered her aunt Marianna best as she had been on the day of Polly's christening, a small, plump woman with a kind smile, and dark hair which, for all her smoothing, would escape at her temples and the nape of her neck in tiny, round curls. That Sunday she had been wearing a dress of her favourite plum colour, with lots of little frills, and before she had taken the baby up from the cradle, she had turned back her skirt and made a lap on her white embroidered petticoat, 'For fear of accidents,' she had said. . . .

It is a cold, snowy day:

Mrs Finch's best blue velvet bonnet with its posy of artificial primroses was protected by the umbrella; but her husband's Sunday top-hat soon looked like that of a snow man, and, by squinting upwards, Charity could see snowflakes hanging on the grey fur edging of her bonnet. . . .

After they had passed the *Magpie* one other churchgoer appeared. It was Luke Atwell, a stocky, red-faced youth of eighteen, who had been asked to stand godfather to the baby. He was waiting for them at his mother's gate, dressed, most unsuitably for the weather, in his all-the-year-round reach-me-down suit of pale grey, with a brand new bright magenta necktie, bought specially for the occasion. His large red hands hung bare by his sides and his peaked cloth cap was but poor protection for his carefully oiled and parted crop of light flaxen hair; but he looked so well pleased with his appearance that it seemed almost cruel of Charity's father to say, 'Surely you're not going out in this weather in that rig-out? Where's your top-coat, man? You'll need it before you get back.' Luke, ever obedient to the voice of authority, even when, as now, the authority was that of age alone, went back indoors and reappeared wearing the old black waterproof he wore at his work. It was the only overcoat he possessed, and that, like his suit, had become too small for him. 'Button up the collar, or you'll get a sore throat,' advised Mrs Finch, and, obedient still, though reluctant, poor Luke extinguished the glory of his bright new tie. Why did not grown-up people understand a person's feelings better, thought Charity.

The service proceeds:

Mrs Truman unwound the wrappings of the bundle on her lap, first peeling off the best Paisley shawl in which Charity and her elder cousins had gone to their christenings, then the large white woolly shawl, then the small knitted one, and revealed the baby in long, lacy robes with blue ribbon bows on the shoulders. The impression this transformation scene should have made was ruined by the smallness of the congregation. Besides the christening party, there were but about a dozen in church, mostly men and boys, and there was none of the rustling and peering and 'pretty dearing' usual on such occasions.

Higher up the social scale the clothes of both baby and adults were naturally more elegant, though the principles remained the same. The eldest son of Mary Hamilton was born on 28 September 1900.

Four weeks later, in Milton Church, our child was christened Richard James Eaglescliffe Erskine by our dear friend, Mr Radcliffe. He wore the robe made for him by Ruth Cawley, with a long cloak of corded silk – a gift from my aunt Emily and a bonnet with a tiny plume on it, and over his face a lace veil. Neither the solemnity of the occasion, nor the formality of Robert's frock coat and silk hat, nor the splendour of my own finery – a dress of blue voile over cream silk, a grey stole and a little hat of cream panne velvet with a cluster of tiny ostrich plumes on one side – subdued Richard. When the water was sprinkled and the Sign of the Cross made on his brow, he bawled vigorously.

The robe in question was 'of the finest lawn, very long, with a bodice composed of minute rows of Valenciennes lace; and, to wear under it, a slip, ornamented with lace and tucks done with tiny feather-stitching'. It was copied from one that was alleged to have been in the Cawley family for three hundred years; but although the tradition is attractive and the robe sounds beautiful, it cannot in fact have been much older than a hundred years. Mary's second child, a daughter, died in infancy. When her third was born, she may have felt superstitious about using the same robe again, for this time she decided to make her own, though still in very much the same style: 'I had made a christening robe of lawn and Valenciennes lace all finely tucked; a filmy garment of which Mrs Powersfort remarked, "It might have been blown together."'

In 1897 Sybil Marshall, then aged seven, was christened together with her brother and sister, and their cousin Jubilee Anne. In her *Fenland Chronicle* she recalls the outfits she and her sister wore for the occasion:

My sister and me had black velvet frocks for the occasion, and I were as proud as a peacock 'cos I had a proper little bustle at the back. It were made like a little square pincushion about nine inches long and four or five inches wide, and I tied it round my waist afore putting my frock on. Then we had black velvet poke bonnets underlined with blue satin, and tied underneath our chins with a big blue satin bow. We set in a row in a pew that were generally used by a big farmer and his family, and when old Parson Harper come down out of his pulpit we all got up and trooped down the church to the font one after the other like ducks to the pond. Mother took our bonnets off and laid 'em on the nearest seat, and there we stood with our faces all turned up while the old man christened our baby cousin, and then dipped the water on us. I remember it all well enough, and it seems that Dad (I shall have to call him that – it comes so ready after all these years) remembered it an' all. He'd be seventeen then, but he must 'a bin a bit different from the general run o' young men, for it seems as he took notice of us little girls and has told me many times that I never looked more beautiful than I did then.

The years following the Great War saw a change in the dress of babies. As the *Big Book of Needlecraft* proclaimed, around 1930: 'Gone are the "long clothes" in which our mothers took so much pride. Those weighty and cumbersome garments are to-day considered very unhygenic. The aim in baby clothes is to have them light, warm, roomy, and just about 27 inches long.' Certainly the trailing robe dear to the Victorians had disappeared, but most mothers still wanted something very special for the christening, and this usually meant a traditional garment. A layette edition of the *Jardin des Modes* for 1935 offered paper patterns in several designs. All have the standard high waist and long skirt, and two have the customery panel of decoration at centre front, but in one of them the traditional ingredients have been interpreted in a very contemporary style: the skirt consists of three overlapping bias-cut flounces, each cut into rounded scallops at the hem, and the waist seam is also scalloped. The thirties were a time of enthusiastic home knitting, and *Woman's Magazine* of 1932 offered a pattern for a complete christening outfit in combined knitting and crochet, worked in fine blue and white wool. 'All readers who decide to make this Robe, Cap and Matinee cannot fail to be delighted with its delicate, lacy charm,' promised the Editor. The robe has a square neck and a high waist slotted with satin ribbon, and frilly openwork sleeves. All three garments are trimmed with appliqué blue crochet flowers and narrow blue stripes.

During the Second World War the prevailing austerity coupled with the system of clothes rationing meant that few people could have gone out and bought a robe specially for a christening. Nevertheless for those who could spare the money and the coupons such robes were available. One of them is preserved in the Gallery of English Costume in Manchester. Although it is exceedingly plain compared with christening robes of earlier periods, some effort has been made to keep it traditional. It is of white rayon satin, 27 inches long, with a high waist and small puffed sleeves. The skirt, which has three horizontal tucks round the hem, is shirred on to the bodice, which is decorated with rows of pulled threads. It bears the Utility mark. The Utility scheme, which was in operation from 1942 to 1951, was not just the Government's safeguard against extravagant use of materials; it was also a guarantee of quality for the consumer, which perhaps explains why so many articles bearing the mark are still around today. At a time when many mothers had to rely on the relief parcels of baby clothes sent over from the United States in order to clothe their babies at all, a dress like this one must have seemed the height of luxury. Perhaps more typical of the period was the garment worn by the daughter of a Merchant Navy officer at her christening in Liverpool in October 1942. She was dressed in a gown put together out of a bolster slip and a pair of net curtains.

For Martha Martin, stranded alone in Alaska when her baby was born, makeshifts were also the order of the day. She was inspired by the memory of her son's baptism: 'Lloyd's christening dress was of fine batiste with many tucks, two rows of spider-web insertion, and wide spider-web lace on the bottom. It was so long it came to Don's knees when we carried him high.' For little Donnas she made a wrap out of the skin of a sea otter she had killed: 'It's a lovely skin, the softest, silkiest, thickest fur I have ever seen. I am going to make a robe for my baby out of the beautiful fur. My darling child may be born in a lowly cabin, but she shall be wrapped in one of the earth's most costly furs.' For days she worked at the fur, stretching it, and then rubbing and pounding it until it was soft and pliable. Then she turned her attention to the other garments, cutting up her own petticoat to make a dress and slip, and unravelling part of a red sock so as to use the wool to embroider the dress with cross-stitch. At last she was able to write with satisfaction: 'Now my child will be properly dressed for her christening. . . . Her dress is made from her mother's garments and her robe is of sea-otter fur.'

In the 1950s the old traditions were reasserted. At Malcolm Annett's christening in Miss Read's *Village Diary*, 'Mrs Moffat had made the christening gown – a miracle of tiny stroked gathers and finely-pleated tucks, with a froth of old lace at the hem.' The guests had all dressed up according to their lights: 'Ted, Mr Annett's brother, was resplendent in his best grey suit and the other godfather was in uniform. . . . Mrs Pringle had come to the service with her cherry-decorated hat on, and a

Christening outfits from *La Layette du Jardin des Modes,* 1935

very dashing white organdie blouse which had once been Mrs Partridge's and had been the *pièce de résistance* at a recent jumble sale.'

As for today, there is no fixed rule. *Debrett's* comments that dress at christenings tends to be elaborate, and rules that women should wear hats and men suits. As for the baby, it notes simply that 'christening robes are by ancient tradition always white and often they are handed down through several generations'. Actually many modern christenings are thoroughly informal, the child, particularly if it is past infancy, being dressed in its ordinary 'best' clothes and the adults attired suitably for church but less formally than for a wedding. A lot depends on the age of the child. Many people feel uneasy about dressing any but the tiniest baby boy in a long, frilly white robe, which may make him look most inappropriately girlish. The current Mothercare range caters for both sexes with a knitted christening romper in white acrylic with an embroidered yoke, and a robe with matching bonnet in white polyester cotton broderie anglaise, as well as a pair of white satin 'christening bootees' with bows and ankle-ties to complete the outfit. They come in one size, to fit a baby from three to nine months – a clear indication of the current average age for christening. They are very reasonably priced, and are doubtless a popular buy for anyone not lucky enough to have access to an antique robe, and without the skill and enthusiasm to make a new one. Families who do possess Victorian robes, or can afford to buy them from antique shops (at upwards from £50 a time), may find them far too small unless they make a point of having their babies christened very promptly. The present writer's first and third sons, christened at four and five months, wore Edwardian day dresses – still splendidly elaborate by modern standards, but ample enough to accommodate them; while the second, who was an energetic fifteen months, wore a navy blue sailor suit specially made for the occasion.

For those who wish to make a robe themselves, sewing, knitting and crochet patterns are all available, and the trimming can be varied to produce an individual result. One very beautiful idea is to make the baby's robe out of the mother's wedding veil, thus producing, for this very special ceremony, a garment rich in associations and symbolism.

6

FOOD

'As we are passing the confectioners' said Mr. Hose to his wife, 'we might tell them to send up a nice sugar cake in honour of baby's Xning.

'Oh yes we might do that' said his wife, scratching her head to show off her net which was carefully covering her knob behind.

They arrived home at last and had the beautiful Xning cake between them for tea.

Angela Ashford, *The Jealous Governes*

The refreshments served at christenings have generally been determined by the taste and purse of the father rather than by any fixed rules or traditions. There is no English equivalent to the French *dragées*, or sugared almonds – pale blue for a boy, pink for a girl – which come in prettily decorated containers and are distributed to the congregation after the service; nor to the cinnamon water, *l'ieau d'cannelle*, which is the traditional christening drink in Jersey. Only one area, the Lake District, seems to have had a speciality to be served on these occasions. This was buttered sops, which were eaten with rum butter. Joseph Budworth recorded a recipe for them in his diary for 1792: 'The bread is cut in thin slices and placed in rows one above the other in a large kettle of 20 or 30 gallons. The butter and sugar are dissolved in a separate one, and then poured upon the bread, where it continues until it has boiled for some space and the bread is perfectly saturated with the mixture. It is then . . . served as a dessert.'

In poorer households the cost of entertaining a lot of people was prohibitive, coming as it did hard upon the expenses of the lying-in itself. In this situation the guests all chipped in with gifts of food. In

Oxfordshire, for example, every woman brought two cakes, one for the
christening party and one for the minister. Across the Channel the same
concept of neighbourly solidarity applied. When Gervaise has her baby
in Zola's *L'Assommoir* the godfather presents her with 6 pounds of sugar
(to build up her strength after her confinement, perhaps), and he and his
wife arrive at the party with two bottles of wine and a large cake bought
from a fashionable *pâtissier*. Doubtless without such contributions it
would have been impossible to have had much of a party, but even the
poorest father usually managed to find the wherewithal to drink the
infant's health. Sabine Baring Gould has given us a description of these
minimal celebrations in *Old Country Life*:

> When a labourer desired to have his child privately baptized, he
> provided a bottle of rum, a pack of cards, a lemon, and a basin of pure
> water, then sent for the parson and the farmer for whom he worked.
> The religious rite over, the basin was removed, the table cleared,
> cards and rum produced, and sat down to. On such occasions the
> rector did not return home till late, and the housekeeper left the
> library window unhasped for the master, but locked the house doors.
> Under the library window was a violet bed, and it was commonly
> reported that the rector had on more than one occasion slept in that
> bed after a christening. Unable to heave up his big body to the sill of
> the window, he had fallen back among the violets, and there slept off
> the exertion.

It is clear that deep drinking on these occasions was the rule rather
than the exception. Parson Woodforde recorded in his diary for 1777
that 'brother John being at the Christening last night being merry
disturbed the whole Company so much that they were obliged to break
up about 11 o'clock'. There is a Cruikshank print of 1864 entitled *The
Worship of Bacchus or The Drinking Customs of Society, Showing, how
Universally the Intoxicating Liquors are used, upon every Occasion in Life, from the
Cradle to the Grave*. The vignette in the centre foreground bears the
heading 'Health to the Young Christian', and shows a group of a dozen
people, all of whom, including two young children, are seen liberally
toasting the infant in claret. A boisterous Australian bush ballad
describes the disastrous result of starting on the drinking before the

ceremony. Maloney has asked the priest to come and baptize all seven of his children:

That night the nine Maloneys, with their neighbours and their cronies,
Sat waiting for the Father, who arrived a little late;
There were lights and water handy (and maybe a drop of brandy)
When Father McInulty's trap pulled up beside the gate.

Their thirst they had abated in the hour that they had waited,
For a christenin needs the comfort of a drop of good potheen;
And Maloney's nose was reddened, and his eyes a trifle deadened,
But 'twas dark within the parlour, and it couldn't well be seen.

Inside Maloney's kitchen all the kids with fun were twitchin'
For to be baptized was something they had never known before;
And a list of names was handed to the Father, who commanded
The evening's operations like a general at the war.

They put the blessed candle in a bottle – 'twas a scandal,
But no other thing to hold it in the farmhouse could be found;
And from Murty up to Paddy all were dragged in by their daddy –
The Holy Church received them; and the baby's turn came round.

Then behold, there was a scuffling, and a grunting, and a snuffling,
And a sudden gust of wind came in and put the candle out.
'Where the divil is that baby?' 'Och, he's on the flagstones, maybe!'
And Maloney picked up something. 'Call him James!' they heard him
                                               shout.

And the Latin words went racing, while Maloney stood embracing
The baby; but he muttered, 'By me sowl, he's pretty big!'
Till Bridget struck a light and screeched out loud in accents frightened
'God save us, holy Father! Ye're baptizin' Murty's pig!'

Perhaps the association with drunkenness partly explains the Puritans' suspicion of christenings. At any rate during the Commonwealth they were officially frowned on, children were registered for the first time under their date of birth not of baptism, and celebrations had to be discreet. John Evelyn attended many christenings, but in his *Diary* he never mentions the social aspect except once, by implication. In 1658 he stood godfather to his nephew George, and noted sourly: 'He was christned the 6t, & on the 7th I came home. Next day I fell ill of the Coliq.' But people managed to enjoy themselves even in those dour times, and we learn from the *Verney Memoirs* that the christening of Betty Alport's baby in 1656 was 'not without a fidler and the merry cup, and the toast of Sir Ralph's health'.

Samuel Pepys went to a great many christenings, and seems on the whole to have had a good time, but for one so interested in his stomach he is strangely reticent about the refreshments. At the christening of Lady Sandwich's daughter Katherine in 1661 he partook of 'a very fine banquet, the best I ever was at', and at the house of Captain and Mrs Ferrers two years later he had 'very pretty and plentiful entertainment', but he goes into no detail. About the party at his cousin Scott's, in 1661, he is even terser: 'Went with the minister into another room and eat and drank.' On subsequent occasions he does refer to getting a piece of cake, and to wine and wafers,* and of one occasion in 1666 he remarks complacently: 'After the christening comes in the wine and the sweetmeats, and then to prate and tattle, and then very good company they were, and I among them.' But not all parties were so enjoyable: in an entry for 1668 Pepys records: '. . . here comes my wife to me, who hath been at Pegg Pen's christening, which, she says, hath made a flutter and noise; but was as mean as could be, and but little company, just like all the rest that that family do'.

Happily other diarists are more expansive. Thomas Turner, an eighteenth-century shopkeeper from Sussex, scrupulously recorded all the refreshments at the christenings he attended, as well as his own degree of sobriety at the end of the evening; though when he speaks of being sober it is hard to tell whether it is with pride or with regret. On one occasion he notes cryptically that 'my wife and I came home about 12.30 and pretty near sober, but something the worse for drinking'. At the christening of the son of William Piper, a neighbouring farmer renowned for his stinginess, Turner describes with virtuous indignation how the guests (of whom he was not one) 'made the poor old man's

---

* These were rich, crisp biscuits. In Georgian times it became fashionable to roll them into a tube shape, thus anticipating the modern brandy-snap.

pocket suffer by . . . emptying as many of his old rusty bottles as they possibly could, and more than their behaviour could give sanction to (as I hear), supposing decency to be the standard for good behaviour'. Three years later, in 1759, Piper asked Turner to stand godfather to another son, but gracelessly excluded Turner's wife from the accompanying invitation to dinner. 'He could not nor would not have the plague and trouble of getting a dinner for so many people, though I believe had not niggardliness been the only motive to prevent his asking his neighbours, there would have been no fear of their coming.' In the event Piper's brother, embarrassed by this discourtesy, persuaded Mrs Turner to join the party, but the occasion was not a happy one.

We, together with Mr. and Mrs. Burges and Mrs. Fuller, dined on a knuckle of pork boiled and greens, a pond currant pudding* and a cold duck pie designed as a pasty. We played at brag in the evening. My wife and I lost 2s. 10d. We stayed and supped with the poor old wretch on a loin of veal which was 4 hours in roasting and then in part roasted, a ham of bacon boiled and greens, the cold duck pasty, a hot buttered apple pie and a hot baked rice pudding, in company with Mr. and Mrs. Porter, Tho. Fuller and his wife, Joseph Fuller and his wife, Mr. Burges and his wife, John Vine and his wife, Joseph Durrant and his wife, Mr. French and his wife, Mr. Calverley and Miss Tealing and Tho. Diplock. [A surprisingly large party if Piper was really so mean.] We came home about 2.40, and all sober. My wife and I gave the nurse and maid 3s. A very dear nights's entertainment, and I am sure a very bad one, for I never spent an evening with less pleasure in my life. There was not any liquor I suppose worth drinking, though I tasted only some small beer and that came like drops of blood.

Other occasions were more enjoyable. When Turner stood godfather to Farmer Carman's daughter Susanna, in 1762, the celebration dinner consisted of 'a leg of lamb boiled, a roasted pig, 4 chicken roasted, a boiled ham, a currant suet pudding and a plain flour pudding, carrots

---

* Pond pudding is a Sussex speciality consisting of a suet crust encasing a whole lemon and a quantity of sugar, which render themselves into a sauce when the pudding is boiled.

and cabbage', and Turner's enjoyment of it was clearly heightened by the thought of 'my family at home dining on the remains of yesterday's dinner with some French beans'. He stayed on to drink tea, and came home 'about 8.15, as sober as when I went from home'. Almost exactly a year later he stood godfather again, this time to Molly Bannister, the daughter of his next-door neighbour, an excise officer. Perhaps that July was hotter than the year before, for the meal they enjoyed was a decidedly summery one of 'a piece of cold roast beef, some cold roast chickens, tart, custards and a piece of cold bacon'. Again Turner stayed to drink tea, and came home 'about 9.40, very sober', while his servant at home made do with the day before's leftovers.

Not all the parties Turner attended were so lavish. His one-time best friend Thomas Davy, a shoemaker and of lower social pretensions than himself, had a little girl six months after a sudden wedding to which Turner was not invited. Davy did, however, 'earnestly solicit' him to attend her christening party. It was clearly a humble affair, the supper consisting of 'bread, cheese and plumcake', but since Turner stayed this time until well after midnight (though still returning sober), it was evidently none the less enjoyable.

Parson Woodforde was another diarist who delighted in recording the details of meals, and in his professional capacity he was frequently asked to christening parties. These ranged from the very simple to the elaborate. In 1763 Woodforde was lodging with Squire Cross of Thurloxton. After he had baptized Cross's son Richard, 'one Farmer Major, of this Parish, spent the afternoon and evening here, drinking with Mr. Cross all the time, neither of them eat any supper, and I left them drinking when I went to bed, which was about 10'. A couple of years later he records that after christening little Mary Burge, 'from church I went to Seth Burge's, where I dined, spent the afternoon, supped and spent the evening', adding mournfully, 'we were to have had a Ham and Fowls for dinner there, but the maid forgot to boil the Ham'. Woodforde christened several children for Squire Custance of Ringland, once at such short notice that he was unable to accept the invitation to dinner, which must have grieved him, for the year before (1780) he had attended a particularly enjoyable party there, of which he recorded every detail:

[The Squire] asked me to dine with the Company at Ringland at 2 o'clock, therefore I walked by myself there and dined and spent the afternoon and stayed till after 7 in the evening and then walked back home. . . . We had for dinner a Calf's Head, boiled Fowl and Tongue, a Saddle of Mutton rosted on the Side Table, and a fine Swan rosted with Currant Jelly Sauce for the first Course. The Second Course a couple of Wild Fowl called Dun Fowls, Larks, Blamange, Tarts etc. etc. and a good Desert of Fruit after amongst which was a Damson Cheese. I never eat a bit of Swan before, and I think it good eating with sweet sauce. The Swan was killed 3 weeks before it was eat and yet not the lest bad taste in it.

In marked contrast to Woodforde's ingenuous enjoyment of the good things in life whenever they chanced to come his way, we have the remorseful outpourings of William Jones, Vicar of Broxbourne. On Christmas Day, 1806, presumably in the aftermath of a colossal hangover, he wrote:

I am thoroughly convinced, – 0! that I had always prudence and resolution enough to act agreeably to my conviction! – that, if we wish to enjoy what are called the good things, & pleasures, of this life, we must use them moderately. Every excess & irregularity tends to destroy enjoyment.

I was at a Christening dinner at Mr. Cozens's on Tuesday last, – & a very grand & expensive entertainment it was. The guests were so numerous that we were almost *pinioned* during dinner-time. Such dinners and jollifications may be very pleasant at the moment; but they cannot be otherwise than hurtful to the feelings of a Christian. My mind seldom recovers its tone for many days afterwards. I am often, particularly after such occasions, almost weary of my life, & wish myself fairly out of it; but I am still more tired of my own weakness & imprudence.

The christening dinner to which Dickens's Mr Dombey treated his guests scarcely qualified as a jollification, though all the requisite ingredients were present:

They found Mr. Pitt turning up his nose at a cold collation, set forth in a cold pomp of glass and silver, and looking more like a dead dinner lying in state than a social refreshment. . . .

'Mr. John,' said Mr. Dombey, 'will you take the bottom of the table, if you please. What have you got there, Mr. John?'

'I have got a cold fillet of veal here, sir,' replied Mr. Chick, rubbing his numbed hands hard together. 'What have *you* got there, sir?'

'This', returned Mr. Dombey, 'is some cold preparation of calf's head, I think. I see cold fowls - ham - patties - salad - lobster. Miss Tox will do me the honour of taking some wine? Champagne to Miss Tox.'

There was a toothache in everything. The wine was so bitter cold that it forced a little scream from Miss Tox, which she had great difficulty in turning into a 'Hem!' The veal had come from such an airy pantry, that the first taste of it had struck a sensation as of cold lead to Mr. Chick's extremities. Mr. Dombey alone remained unmoved. He might have been hung up for sale at a Russian fair as a specimen of a frozen gentleman.

The prevailing influence was too much even for his sister. She made no effort at flattery or small talk, and directed all her efforts to looking as warm as she could.

'Well, sir,' said Mr. Chick, making a desperate plunge, after a long silence, and filling a glass of sherry; 'I shall drink this, if you'll allow me, sir, to little Paul.'

'Bless him!' murmured Miss Tox, taking a sip of wine.

'Dear little Dombey!' murmured Mrs. Chick. . . .

The Bloomsbury christening in *Sketches by Boz* was altogether different, and but for the presence of the killjoy godfather Dumps, all the guests would have considered it a thorough success, making up in jollity for what it lacked in sophistication. Three dozen or so guests enjoyed singing, dancing and cards, and partook of bon-bons, rout-cakes and negus, whose smell of nutmeg, almonds and port wafted right out on to the staircase. There was a sit-down supper in the parlour, which the Kitterbells clearly intended to be rather impressive, for they had hired the services of the local greengrocer to act as footman, and had indulged in some ambitious table decorations:

There were four barley-sugar temples on the table, which would have looked beautiful if they had not melted away when the supper began; and a water-mill, whose only fault was that, instead of going round, it ran over the table-cloth. Then there were fowls, and tongue, and trifle, and sweets, and lobster salad, and potted beef – and everything. And little Kitterbell kept calling out for clean plates, and the clean plates did not come; and then the gentlemen who wanted the plates said they didn't mind, they'd take a lady's; and then Mrs. Kitterbell applauded their gallantry, and the greengrocer ran about till he thought his seven-and-sixpence was very hardly earned; and the young ladies didn't eat much, for fear it shouldn't look romantic, and the married ladies ate as much as possible, for fear they shouldn't have enough; and a great deal of wine was drunk, and everybody talked and laughed considerably.

The Victorian age saw a trend away from the substantial form of christening entertainment consisting of early afternoon dinner followed by supper, coffee and tea, with accompanying alcoholic drinks. The very rich and ostentatious may have taken the opportunity to hold a ball, but

a dialogue in *The Ladies' Treasury* of the 1860s makes it clear that right-thinking people deplored such extravagance:

> GERALDINE: I think of giving a ball in honour of baby's christening, mamma.
>
> MRS. VERNON: A ball is the last thing I should advocate to celebrate so holy an event. What have the frivolous people brought together by a ball to do with the joyful yet solemn change wrought by baptism in the prospects of your darling? A ball, such as you would be expected to give, would cost at least three hundred pounds. Can you not employ that sum in some charitable donation to the poor of the parish?

Few people were in a position to contemplate such a lavish scale of entertainment, however, and the most popular course was to give an afternoon tea-party. A typical Victorian christening tea might consist of assorted sandwiches, buttered pikelets, shortbread, queen cakes, *petits-fours* and christening cake. Now the cake became the focal point of the proceedings. Traditional christening cake was filled with fruit and retained its rich flavour for a good spell. In these respects it resembled wedding cake, and it must be from this time that the custom dates of keeping the top tier of the wedding cake to serve at the christening. Mrs Beeton gives a recipe for 'Bride or Christening Cake', in keeping with the usual lavish scale of her cookery (see Appendix 3, pp. 159–60).

Those who were daunted by the prospect of spending over an hour beating a cake as hard as possible, as the recipe stipulates, could order it ready-made from Harrod's or the Army & Navy Stores, 'ornamented to suit the requirements of customers'. The weight ranged from 3 to 20 pounds and the cost was a shilling per pound in 1895, rising to 1*s*. 3*d*. in 1913, so rather better value than Mrs Beeton's recipe, though perhaps not so rich. It was usual for the decorations to include a tiny cradle: these could be bought from the above-mentioned shops for between 1*s*. and 3*s*. When Mary Hamilton had her first son christened in 1900, 'Richard's godmother gave the christening cake which was decorated with shamrocks, roses and thistles and a miniature cradle in the centre'. The cake had by now become the one indispensable feature of even the most minimal celebration: when Richard's sister was christened four

Edwardian christening cake

years after him, their parents had recently been posted to a new area.
'None of our relations were present and we knew few people in
Folkestone; but two elderly ladies who lived next door came in to tea to
admire little Louise, and to taste a morsel of her christening cake.'

In humbler circles, although the cake was an important item, a solid
meal was still favoured. The miner's family in D.H. Lawrence's story

The Christening, round about 1914, sit down to 'a great spread on the table, of tinned fruits and tinned salmon, ham and cakes', and Flora Thompson has left us a delightful description of a late-nineteenth-century christening party in a farm bailiff's family:

Soon they were all in the big, warm living kitchen, their damp outer garments removed, and their faces, burnished by a rough towelling, reflecting the blaze of the fresh log Bess had thrown on the embers. The blaze shone on the brightly-coloured crockery on the dresser shelves and the brass candlesticks and red-and-white pottery dogs on the mantelpiece and lighted up the festive-looking tea-table, which had been left ready spread with the best china and with dishes of bread and butter and scones and jam and, to crown all, in the middle, the christening cake which, the day before, Charity's mother had iced and inscribed in pink sugar piping: *Mary Alice*.

But there was a surprise to come. When, in the semi-privacy of the chimney-corner, Mrs. Truman had fed Mary Alice with food more suitable to her age than iced cake and laid her in her cradle, 'Now, Bess,' she said. 'Look sharp with the forks and spoons.' Then, to the company at large, 'You'll never guess what I've got for your teas.'

Her sister, with her head on one side, studied the forks and spoons Bess was placing on the table, then said in the conventionally reproachful tone called for in such circumstances, 'You've never gone and cooked a ham?' 'No,' said her sister. 'It's not ham; nothing so common. It's something you've never heard of for tea before, christening or no christening. But you wait a minute and you'll see', and, after girding herself with a white apron, she went out to the back kitchen and soon reappeared carrying a pudding of noble proportions. 'Now, pass your plates,' she said, seating herself at table. 'I'm not going to tell you what's in it; you must find out', and she stuck her knife into the rich, flaky suet crust, releasing a stream of brown gravy, and began to spoon generous helpings on to the plates.

'You could make a good meal on the smell alone,' said Charity's father, sniffing the air appreciatively. But what was that within the pudding that smelt so delicious? It was not beef, for it was cut into joints, and the joints were not those of a rabbit. Charity's parents looked puzzled. Luke was licking his lips and staring round-eyed.

Then, as Mrs. Finch began cutting up Charity's portion, she exclaimed, 'Upon my soul, our Marianna, I do believe it's a fowl! Who ever heard of such extravagance!' And Marianna said modestly, 'I thought you'd all be as hungry as hunters this cold day, so I got Reuben to kill a couple of those cockerels. . . .'

If her guests had not felt hungry before, the sight and smell of the cockerel pudding had given them good appetites. In a very short time the last remnant of suet crust, with the last scraping of gravy and oddments of pork, were being spooned on to Luke's plate to accompany the last pickings of his drumstick. Then every vestige of the meat course was cleared from the table by Bess. 'Take pepper and salt and everything,' her mother said. 'Then I'll cut the cake. We must have a genteel tea-table when Mrs. Pocock and Stella come in. . . .'

After Mrs. Pocock and Stella had retired to their own part of the house, the christening party drew into a circle round the fire and the men drank beer, heated by thrusting down into the hot coals the point of a long, conical vessel there known as a hooter, while the women and girls sipped elderberry wine and ate hot roasted chestnuts. Luke held the shovel containing the chestnuts over the fire and when they were roasted handed them round in strict rotation, though the largest and best-cooked nuts seemed always to fall to Bess's share, and these, before passing them to her, he shelled. His face was almost as red as the live coals and sweat glistened upon his brow, but his broad smile betokened pure happiness.

Mary Alice was christened at the afternoon service, but most christenings took place in the morning. If a tea-party was to be held later, there was the problem of how to fill in the time in between. In her book *Little Entertainments and How to Manage Them* (1904), Mrs Waldemar Leverton advised that the ceremony

. . . should be followed by a little luncheon, to which one would naturally invite the god-parents and the officiating clergyman. . . . After luncheon the hostess would be quite justified in taking an hour's rest before the other guests arrive, her husband devoting himself to the entertainment of the god-parents and others, who naturally being old friends, or perhaps relatives, would not expect to be treated with ceremony.

For this essentially simple and informal meal she suggests a summer menu of prawns in aspic, salmon mayonnaise, veal and ham pie and salad, followed by gooseberry fool, vanilla cream, tartlets, fruit and cheese; or a winter one of oysters, clear soup, roast fowl with artichokes and potatoes, hot apple tart, marron purée à la Chantilly, cheese, dessert and coffee, 'while for table decoration a silver basket, or one of fancy wicker-work, with a large white satin bow on the handle, filled with white blossoms, would be quite sufficient'.

For the tea-party itself, which she envisages lasting from 4 p.m. to 6 or 7, she recommends a buffet tea in the dining-room, with rather more elaborate decorations: 'A very charming effect would be to arrange the entire centre of the table to look like a small lake by means of plate glass, edged with hemlock green, while laid upon the mirror might be arranged water lilies in their season. Little white ornaments displaying Cupids would hold fronds of ferns and sprays of blossom.' As for the food,

> . . . the christening cake should hold the place of honour. This is cut by the mother of the baby during the afternoon, and champagne should be provided to drink the infant's health. For ordinary refreshments the hostess would provide sandwiches, cakes, brown and white bread and butter, with tea, coffee, lemonade, claret, and champagne cup. Fruit, too, might also be added if preferred, but this is not necessary. The guests should not stay the entire time, half-an-hour being quite long enough to remain on these occasions.

Debrett's Etiquette and Modern Manners remarks that christening parties today are generally small and informal, and considers a lunch-, tea- or early evening drinks party all equally suitable, depending on the time of the ceremony. With a growing trend for baptisms to be integrated into the normal Sunday morning service, at least in the Church of England, lunches are perhaps the most common. Helen Cox's book *Mr and Mrs Charles Dickens Entertain at Home* gives recipes and menus taken from Kate Dickens's own cookery book as well as modern counterparts. Her suggestion for a present-day tea is substantially the same as the

Victorian one quoted earlier, though with the substitution of cheese and bacon savouries and coffee sponge cake for the pikelets and *petits-fours*. She also gives a menu for a high tea, consisting of christening cake, date and walnut scones, muffins and sliced bread and butter, cold meats and assorted salads, apple shortcake and pineapple upside-down cake. Nowadays most people still choose the rich fruit variety for the christening cake, covered with marzipan and royal icing, though if the guests include a lot of children a light sponge may be preferred. The most common decoration, apart from the child's name and the date written in icing, is a stork, with or without a baby in a napkin hanging from its beak, though many people prefer a tiny open Bible made of fondant icing, with a blue or pink ribbon marker.

When Martha Martin gave birth to her baby, totally alone and miles from any other human life, as we saw in an earlier chapter, she was determined that her daughter should have not just a baptism but a celebration as well, even if there were only animals with which to share it. And she spent days of planning and preparation:

I have opened cans of fruit and vegetables and the one can of olives. I dug under the puncheon and got the last of the carrots from our garden and all the marble-size potatoes, which I'll give to the deer. I got bigger spuds from off the boat for myself, scrubbed them thoroughly, and greased them ready to bake. I also peeled an onion. Only seven onions are left.

The dishpan is full of cut-up bread, just the size to throw to the deer. All the tiny potatoes and about half the carrots are in pails, ready for me to carry to the beach.

I cooked another ptarmigan; though I haven't eaten any of it yet, I did have a cup of hot broth. The feast is ready and waiting, and the guests know they are to come, because I've been giving them samples for a week. They hang around all the time, and they have told me they wouldn't think of missing the christening feast.

When the day came, Donnas was baptized in the sea, watched by the deer who had come to find the bits of scattered bread:

Since it was Baby's party, she got her feast first, and she went to sleep taking it. I let her sleep for a while, then wrapped her in the fur robe, took more food, and went out to our guests, who were still hanging around, patiently waiting for more hand-outs. . . . Baby and I sat down and served the feast. The jays were there with all their relatives. I told my little one there would always be a rabble in the world, but the rabble, too, must be fed. I threw bread to the jays, and did not grudge it. . . .

The deer stayed close by, some of them not too well mannered. Some were greedy, stamping their feet at one another, grunting, laying back their ears; all of them licking their chops. I kept throwing them food until there was no more. Then I sang, 'Come, Thou fount of every blessing, tune my heart to sing Thy praise,' and 'Jesus, tender Shepherd, hear me. Bless Thy little Lamb!'

The christening ceremony was ended, and we went back into the cabin.

7

ROYAL CHRISTENINGS

O lord archbishop,
Thou hast made me now a man! never, before
This happy child, did I get any thing.
This oracle of comfort has so pleas'd me,
That when I am in heaven I shall desire
To see what this child does, and praise my Maker.
I thank ye all. To you, my good lord mayor,
And your good brethren, I am much beholding:
I have receiv'd much honour by your presence,
And ye shall find me thankful. Lead the way, lords,
Ye must all see the queen, and she must thank ye,
She will be sick else. This day, no man think
Has business at his house; for all shall stay:
This little one shall make it holiday.
William Shakespeare, Henry VIII

'It is usual', observed the author of *Enquire Within Upon Everything* primly in 1865, 'to make a christening the occasion of festivity; but not in such a manner as to require special remark.' Royal christenings have differed from ordinary ones chiefly in being deliberately ostentatious. There were legitimate reasons for this: to the parents' personal feelings of joy and thankfulness were added weightier dynastic considerations, so that the birth of a first-born son to a ruling monarch was a matter of interest and importance to the whole country. The tiny baby was already a political figure, and his christening was his first public appearance; his importance had to be symbolized by the sumptuousness of his clothes, by the splendour of the ceremonial and by the magnificence of his gifts. Woe betide the royal infant who lacked the necessary *savoir-faire* on such

115

an occasion. Ethelred II, baptized (by immersion) in about 968, 'defiled the sacrament by a natural evacuation'. Many other babies must have done the same thing without causing more than temporary embarrassment to their parents, but this baby was royal, which lent a graver aspect to the whole episode, and caused the officiating bishop to lose his temper and prophesy that 'By God, and His mother, this will be a sorry fellow.' Although it was not this particular incident that earned the King the epithet 'Unready', the bishop's prophecy was as near the mark as could be, the King's long reign bringing a series of unmitigated disasters.

Prince Arthur, the eldest son of Henry VII and Elizabeth of York, was born prematurely on 20 September 1486. Four days later he was baptized in Winchester Cathedral. His aunt, Cecily, Lady Welles, carried him to the font wrapped in a mantle of crimson cloth of gold, lined with ermine, with a long train which was carried by the Marchioness of Dorset, helped by Sir John Cheyney. Anne of York, another of his aunts, carried the chrisom cloth, which was pinned on her right breast and hung over her left arm. His godmother was his grandmother, Elizabeth Wydeville, who presented him with a rich covered cup of gold. Arthur's sister Margaret, born on 29 November 1489, was baptized at Westminster the following day, and her aunt Anne again carried the chrisom cloth, 'with a marvellous rich cross lace'. The baby's godmother was the Countess of Richmond, who gave her a small silver-gilt box filled with gold. The King's children were all baptized in the font of Canterbury Cathedral, which had to be specially transported for the purpose, at a fee of 6s. 8d. to the bearer and £2 to the servant of the Prior of Christ Church at Canterbury. It had then to be suitably installed and decorated, according to the Ordinances laid down for royal christenings: 'The Font must be set on hight that the pepill may see the cristenynge and presse not to ny; and the Font must be hangid with a rich sele [canopy] and overlaid about with carpets on the greces [steps] and other places; and the Font must be hangide all about with clothe of golde and laid withine withe small lyn clothe.'

Although Princess Elizabeth, born in 1533, was not the male heir Henry VIII and Anne Boleyn longed for, her christening was nevertheless celebrated with great splendour. It took place in the Chapel of the Observant Franciscans at Greenwich, and the guests who included, in addition to the usual nobles and church dignitaries, Sir Stephen

Peacocke, Lord Mayor of London, and forty of the chief citizens, arrived in barges. Sir Stephen was dressed in crimson velvet and the aldermen in scarlet, with all the insignia of their office. From the landing-stage to the chapel, the way was hung with tapestries and strewn with fresh rushes, and the procession filed along two by two to the sound of trumpets. The baby was carried by her godmother, the Duchess of Norfolk, who wore a rich mantle of purple velvet lined with ermine, so long and heavy that three people had to hold it up. Four lords walked on either side of her, supporting a canopy; Lady Mary of Norfolk carried the chrisom cloth, which was encrusted with pearls and jewels. The chapel was hung with arras, and the silver font, covered with a fine cloth, was surmounted by a crimson canopy fringed with gold, and gentlemen wearing aprons and towels about their necks stood round it to make sure that no impurities should taint the water. A screen had been erected, behind which stood a brazier, and beside it the Princess was undressed before being immersed and baptized by her godfather, Archbishop Cranmer. Immediately this had been done two hundred torches were lit up and Garter King of Arms proclaimed: 'God of His infinite goodness send prosperous life and long to the high and mighty Princess Elizabeth.' Then the procession made its way back to the palace where Anne Boleyn, lying in state in a crimson velvet mantle lined with ermine, heard all about the ceremony and was shown the christening gifts – a standing cup of gold from Cranmer, another, fretted with pearl, from the Duchess of Norfolk, and three pounced gilt bowls with a cover from the Marchioness of Dorset.

If even Elizabeth, an unwelcome girl, could be christened with such a show of splendour, it is not surprising that the christening of her half-brother Edward four years later should have been an occasion of almost hysterical jubilation. Here at last, after twenty-eight years, was the son Henry and the entire nation had longed for, the son who was to ensure the royal succession and maintain the strength of the monarchy. Everything about his christening, which took place at Hampton Court on 15 October 1537, when he was three days old, was designed to assert his supreme importance. Unfortunately plague was rife in some parts of the country, and precautions had to be taken. Certain areas were banned from sending any representatives at all, and attempts were made to limit the total number of guests. Dukes might not bring more than six gentlemen in their entourage, nor marquesses more than five, and bishops were restricted to three chaplains. The assembled company still numbered three or four hundred, and poor Queen Jane, who had been delivered by Caesarean section three days before and had only another nine days to live, received them all, propped up on a State bed beside Henry, wrapped in velvet and fur. Then the torch-lit procession set out from the State bedchamber to the chapel. Noblemen, churchmen, statesmen, foreign ambassadors, were followed by the godfathers – Cranmer again, and the Dukes of Norfolk and Suffolk. The Earls of Sussex and Montagu carried silver basins, the Earl of Wiltshire a wax taper, the Earl of Essex a gold salt-cellar. The four-year-old Princess Elizabeth carried the jewelled chrisom cloth, which was so heavy that she herself had to be carried by Edward Seymour. Lady Exeter carried the baby himself. Three marchionesses held a canopy above her, and two nobles held up her train. Then came the wet-nurse and midwife, also under a canopy, a group of gentlemen with wax tapers, and finally the godmother, Edward's half-sister Mary, and her ladies. The ceremony was performed by Cranmer from a new silver-gilt font and the Prince was washed in a curtained alcove, in warm, perfumed water. Then after a flourish of trumpets, Garter King of Arms again made his proclamation: 'God of His almighty and infinite grace give and grant good life and long to the right high, right excellent and noble Prince, Prince Edward, Duke of Cornwall and Earl of Chester, most dear and most entirely beloved son to our most dread and gracious Lord, King Henry VIII. Largesse, largesse, largesse!' The procession then made its way back to the State bedchamber where Edward was presented to his parents, Henry weeping for joy, and the light from the many torches making it seem like day, although it was in fact by now the middle of the night. The celebrations continued the next day throughout the country and Latimer wrote to Cromwell: 'Here is no less rejoicing at the birth of our Prince, whom we hungered for so long, than there was at the birth of John the Baptist . . . God give us grace to be thankful.'

Magnificent as these celebrations were, they seem a touch provincial when compared with similar occasions on the Continent. Queen Claude, the wife of Henry's French contemporary François I, gave birth to a son on 28 February 1518, and he was christened in the château of Amboise on 25 April. It was a brilliant and cosmopolitan gathering. The godfather was Lorenzo de' Medici, Duke of Urbino and nephew to the Pope. He carried the child, who was wrapped in a mantle of cloth of silver lined with ermine, the four corners being held up by the Comte de Guise, the Marquis of Mantua, the Prince of Orange and the Duke of Albany. The procession made its way from the royal chamber, across a bridge lined with rich carpets and lit with huge white wax tapers in golden holders, into the church which was all hung with cloth of gold and silver. The baptism was performed by Cardinal de Boisy, and as soon as it was over fanfares were sounded. Afterwards there was a magnificent banquet, masquerades and dancing. The courtyard of the château, hung with tapestries showing classical and biblical scenes, was filled with tents, brilliantly lit by innumerable candles. The decorations had been designed by Leonardo. The celebrations ended triumphantly with the knighting of the baby by the national hero, Bayard.

In 1566 Mary Queen of Scots gave birth to her son James. Determined that he should have every advantage she could procure for him, she set about planning a brilliant christening. The godparents were the King of France, the Duke of Savoy and Queen Elizabeth of England. The ceremony took place in the Chapel Royal at Stirling Castle on 17 December, and James was baptized according to the Catholic rite in the great gold font that weighed 2 stones, which was a present from his godmother. The Prince, who was at the unusually advanced age of six months, was carried by torchlight to the chapel, followed by a procession of Catholic nobles bearing the adjuncts of the ceremony, and received by the Archbishop of St Andrews. The godparents were all represented by proxies, which was by no means unusual – the Comte de Brienne for the French king, M. du Croc for the Duke, and the Earl of Bedford for Elizabeth. Unfortunately the Catholic rite went against Bedford's Puritan conscience, so he and the Scottish Protestant lords stood outside the chapel while it went on, the Countess of Argyll having to stand proxy for the proxy and actually hold the child at the font. After the ceremony came the entertainments, which Mary laid on unstintingly, dressing her nobles for the occasion at her own expense in cloth of gold and silver. Taxes of £12,000 were levied to pay for the fireworks, masques and dancing in which all, even those in Bedford's entourage, participated. The only mishap was during one of the masques, when a group of French satyrs was felt to have made deliberately insulting gestures towards the English, but otherwise everything went well. After the festivities the English party went home. Sir James Melville, Mary's envoy to the court of Elizabeth, recorded that

> . . . my Lord of Bedford was rewarded with a rich chain of diamonds, worth 2000 crowns; Mr. Carey with a chain of pearl and a ring with a fair diamond; Mr. Hatton had a chain with Her Majesty's picture, and a ring; Mr. Lignish and five others of quality had all chains. I was commanded with many others to attend them to the boundary road. They parted all very well content and satisfied with the Queen's Majesty.

Mary was clearly determined that whatever else they might say about her, they should not call her mean. She must also have been savouring her temporary triumph over her childless and unmarried English cousin.

When James's own son Henry was born at Stirling, on 19 February 1594, the King wanted his christening to be equally magnificent and international – a justifiable ambition, since the Queen was Danish. In fact it turned into a diplomatic nightmare. James wanted envoys to go to England, Denmark, France and the Lowland States, to invite their ambassadors to the christening, but incompetent men were appointed and the whole mission was carried out with so little tact that almost all the countries involved took offence. The Dutch and Danish ambassadors arrived first. The Dukes of Mecklenburg and Brunswick were sulking because they had not been sent an envoy each, but only one between them, which they resented as an insult. As a result their own envoys refused to travel from Leith to Edinburgh with the Danish ambassador, but insisted on a separate convoy. Once in Edinburgh they had to wait, because the rebuilding of the chapel at Stirling was not yet finished, and because still no word had been received from either France or England, and it fell to the lot of the unfortunate Melville to try to entertain them. At length it was decided to wait no longer, and a day was fixed for the ceremony, at which point news came that the Earl of Sussex was on his way from England – a last-minute decision of Elizabeth's when she heard that France was not participating. So at last the christening took place, France being represented by an empty chair. 'The order of the banquet and triumph I leave to others to set out,' wrote the harassed

Melville. What was lacking in conviviality, however, was made up for in magnificence. The Prince made his appearance in a robe of purple velvet set with pearls, and his escort of noblemen carried among other things a crown set with diamonds, emeralds, rubies and sapphires. And the ambassadors rose handsomely to the occasion when it came to presents:

> Then every one of them, by order, gave their presents for the god-bairn gift. The jewels of precious stones the queen received in her own hand and then delivered them unto me [wrote Melville], to put them again in their cases, and lay them upon a table which was prepared in the midst of the chamber to set them upon. The Queen of England's had a great show, being a fair cupboard of silver overgilt, cunningly wrought, and some cups of massy gold. The ambassadors of the states presented a golden box, wherein was written on parchment, in letters of gold, 'A gift of a yearly pension to the prince of five thousand . . . by year', with great cups of massy gold, two especially which were enough for me to lift and set them down upon the said table. I leave it to others to set down their weight and value.

He added bitterly: 'But I say, these which were of gold, which should have been kept in store to posterity, were soon melted and spent.' When the children of Henri IV and Marie de Médicis of France were christened at Fontainebleau in 1606, the Queen wore a dress for the occasion that was embroidered with thirty-two thousand pearls and three thousand diamonds. If royal expenditure on dress could reach such extremes, it is perhaps not surprising if the christening gifts were sometimes misappropriated.

Not all royal christenings had the desired effect of creating good feeling in the country at large, particularly when they exacerbated existing religious differences. When James II's eldest son, James Francis Edward, was baptized in 1688, the King's choice of godparents for the baby, the Dowager Queen Catherine of Braganza and the Pope, merely increased his unpopularity and the general anti-Catholic feeling. According to the *Verney Memoirs*: 'Abbot Barberini is to bring the consecrated clouts to England; they are 3 suits richly embroidered with gold.' This would appear to have been a gift from the Pope to his godson.

Thirty-two years later, when James's own son, Charles Edward Stuart ('Bonnie Prince Charlie'), was born in Rome on 20 December 1720, the Pope baptized him himself and presented him with 6,000 scudi worth of consecrated baby-linen.

Among the quarrelsome Hanoverians a christening was as good an opportunity as any for a family row, and a spectacular one was prompted by the christening, in 1717, of William, Duke of Cumberland, the second son of the Prince of Wales (later George II). The Prince had intended his father and his uncle to be the godfathers, but the King discovered by careful inquiry that it was his prerogative, in such cases, to name the second godfather. 'Nothing could equal the Prince's indignation', recalled Lord Hervey, 'when the King named the Duke of Newcastle [whom the Prince hated] for the second sponsor, and would hear of no other. The christening took place, as usual, in the Princess's bedchamber. No sooner had the bishop closed the ceremony, than the Prince, crossing the foot of the bed, stepped up to the Duke of Newcastle, and holding up his hand and forefinger in a menacing attitude, said, '*You are a rascal*, but I shall find you'; meaning in broken English, "I shall find a time to be revenged."' Owing to the Prince's strong German accent, Newcastle understood him to say 'I shall fight you', and reported to the King that he had been challenged. Furious, George I put his son under house arrest. This was lifted four days later, but the Prince and Princess were forced to leave St James's Palace and their children were taken from them. A reconciliation was not effected until 1720, and then it was only nominal: father and son hated each other to the last.

Elizabeth, Duchess of Northumberland, has left in her diaries an account of a much happier Hanoverian christening, that of the child who was to become George IV, on 8 September 1762:

Went to Court at half an hour after Six. We waited in Presence Chamber till ye Queen order'd us to come in. It was the prettiest sight I ever saw. At the head of the Drawing Room was a Bed of State of Crimson Velvet trimm'd with Gold lined with White Sattin and adorn'd with Carving, Gilding, & plumes of White Feathers. The Queen was very finely adorned with Jewels of Diamonds & Emeralds, particularly a vast knot which almost covered her Stomacher. Her Dress was White & Silver, the whole Counterpain & Valens of the Bed were covered with Brussels Lace most extremely fine; it cost 3700£. At the Feet on a Table stood a Large Gilt Bowl on High Step & on each side Gilt Flaggons. On the Right Hand nearest the Bed stood Ly. Bolingbroke. . . . Then came the King with all his Household.

The Queen spoke to all the Royal Family, & then the Lord Chamberlain went to fetch the Prince & ultimately return'd preceded by the verger & followed by Ly. C. Finch (Governess to the Prince), bearing the Child on a White Sattin Pillow embroidered with Gold, & follow'd by the rest of his Servants. Then the Princess Dowager took the Prince from Ly. Charlotte (he cry'd most lustily), & the Abp. of Canterbury began the Ceremony of the Baptism, the Sponsors being the Ps. Dowager of Wales, the Duke of Cumberland, & the reigning Duke of Mecklenburg (by his proxy, the D. of Devonshire). The King stood on the left hand of the Archbishop & behaved during the whole Service with the most affecting piety. The Prince was named George Augustus Frederick.

He then return'd to his Apartment & all present congratulated the Queen, after which, being left alone with her Ladys, we assisted her in getting off the Bed & then attended her to her Apartment.

George III's third daughter was christened in 1770, wearing a white satin mantle lined with pink and edged with ermine, set with £1,000 worth of jewels, the whole garment being valued at £2,800. It was quite a job for the guests to live up to such splendour, but clearly it was expected of them. Lady Shelburne, attending a royal christening in 1768, 'was so illuminated with jewels and radiant with gold and silver she must have added splendour even to that magnificent assembly', and at the christening in 1773 of Sophia Matilda, daughter of the Duke of Gloucester, the Duchess of Cumberland wore 'a full dress'd sack of Rose Colour'd Lutestring trimm'd with Point [lace], a Diamond Stomacher, Sleeve Knots, Necklace & Ear Rings & a vast many Diamonds in her Hair'.

Even when the baby and its parents were not royal, the presence (real or by proxy) of royalty at the ceremony invested it with artificial grandeur, as Sarah, Lady Lyttelton recalled:

I perfectly remember all the mummery at royalty-honoured christenings in my day. My dear sister was just so done by [in 1794]. A great, fat, oldish baby she was; and my mother had to lie up after weeks of active health, in white satin and lace wrappers, and making believe she could not get up to receive the lord and lady who came proxies for King George III and Queen Charlotte in the Spencer House ball-room. I was seven years old. My Grandmother Spencer appeared in full dress, which in her case consisted of a complete suit of plain brown silk, worn over a huge hoop. In short, it was all contrived to be as little like a common baptism as possible.

One of the most spectacular royal christenings was that of Napoleon II, the King of Rome, in 1811. His marriage to Josephine having proved childless, Napoleon Bonaparte had divorced her and taken as his second wife the Archduchess Marie-Louise of Austria. Her compatriots regarded her as a sacrificial victim; her husband stated that he was marrying a womb. Despite this unpromising beginning they became extremely fond of each other. She was soon pregnant, and when in the course of her labour the doctors broke it to Napoleon that the baby was the wrong way up and that they would have to use forceps, which meant endangering either mother or child, he had no hesitation in ordering them to save Marie-Louise at all costs. But in the event both she and the baby survived, and Napoleon was overjoyed. Paris and Rome were illuminated, and there were bonfires, firework displays and *Te Deums*. To reconcile the demands of the Church for a speedy baptism, and the State for a showy one, the baby underwent a ceremony of *ondoiement*, or stopgap baptism, in the chapel of the Tuileries on the evening of his birth, 20 March. The room was full of royal relatives and statesmen. As the proud father, carrying his son, drew near to the silver-gilt font on its granite stand, the company fell totally silent and through the windows could be heard the muffled sounds of the milling crowds outside. The public baptism took place at Notre-Dame on 9 June. Bells rang all over Paris, while the endless procession of court carriages took two hours to make its way from the Tuileries to the cathedral. Then came the royal infant in a coach drawn by eight horses. He was sitting on the lap of his governess, Madame de Montesquiou, and wore a robe of Brussels lace with the ribbon of the Légion d'honneur across his chest, and a mantle of gold lined with ermine. Last of all came his parents, Napoleon in purple velvet and gold, Marie-Louise in white satin and diamonds. The ceremony was performed by Cardinal Fesch, the Emperor's uncle; the godparents were the Emperor of Austria, Francis I (the baby's maternal grandfather), represented by his proxy the Grand Duke of Würzburg, the baby's paternal grandmother, and his aunt, Caroline of Naples, represented by Queen Hortense of Holland, Josephine's daughter by her first marriage. As soon as the baptism itself was over, Madame de Montesquiou placed the baby in his mother's arms while, amid cheers, a herald made a threefold proclamation of 'Long live the King of Rome!' Now Napoleon himself took the baby, kissed him on the forehead and the cheeks, and then raised him high above his head while the crowd applauded and the organ thundered. Afterwards, however, as the imperial couple made their way to the banquet at the Hôtel de Ville, they could not fail to be struck by the crowd's lack of enthusiasm: no amount of pageantry could compensate for economic recession and ever-more hard-hitting conscription.

Queen Victoria's christening, in the Cupola Room at Kensington Palace almost exactly eight years later, was the last of the tense, fraught, Hanoverian family gatherings. As we saw in an earlier chapter, her uncle the Prince Regent was determined to make the occasion as unpleasant as possible, and had soon reduced his sister-in-law to audible sobs. The christenings of Victoria's own children were very different. The eldest, Vicky, born on 21 November 1840, was baptized on 10 February 1841, which was her parents' first wedding anniversary. Although it was, inevitably, a formal State occasion, Victoria and Albert wanted everybody to enjoy it as much as possible. It was held in the throne-room at Buckingham Palace. When Albert was told that George Elvey had composed an anthem for the occasion, and was asked at what point it should be sung, he replied: 'Not at all – no anthem. If the service ends by an anthem, we shall all go out criticising the music. We will have something we all know, in which we can all join – something devotional – the "Hallelujah Chorus". We shall all join in that with all our hearts.' He himself certainly threw himself into the preparations with all his heart: it was he who designed the silver-gilt lily font, which was filled with water brought from the River Jordan, and which has been used for royal christenings ever since, and he also designed the cake, which was decorated with figures of Neptune and

The Christening of the Princess Royal at Buckingham Palace, 1841, by C.R. Leslie, RA.
Queen Adelaide is leaning on the table.

Britannia, the latter holding a pink sugar baby in her arms. The
christening robe was of silk and Honiton lace, and like the font it is still
used to this day.

Almost exactly a year later the Prince of Wales was christened in St
George's Chapel, Windsor. This time the celebrations were much more
lavish, in response to the clamouring of the press for a public service. The
cake was 8 feet across, and toasts were drunk from a vast punchbowl
containing thirty dozen bottles of mulled claret. Commemorative mugs
were produced and celebrations were held all over the country. Caroline
Clive mentions in her diary 'a ball at Solihull in honour of the event,
which is to be composed of farmers, tradespeople and servants. The
higher ranks quarrel too much to dance together. Gentleman's tickets
are 4/- and ladies 3/- including tea, etc. and cars to carry the company
to and fro. The surplus is to be given to the poor'. But not everybody

approved of this worldliness. Edward Walpole wrote:

> I am quite scandalized at the Queen wantonly postponing the baptism of the infant POW until the Lord knows what day in February. She seems to forget, or to be ignorant, that baptism is a solemn and sacred Sacrament and not a mere Court Pageant. A sudden convulsive fit may occur and then what will she not have to answer for? . . . If the queen does not know right from wrong, those about her should set her right, for a Sovereign may not indulge in whims and caprices which would be immaterial in a subject of private station.

A letter from Sarah, Lady Lyttelton, governess to the royal children, suggests that the splendour of the occasion was not without its disadvantages:

> I am very sorry indeed you expect a descriptive letter from me; I have not an atom of description to give. My own 'personal memories' of the christening consisted in being squeezed very close between the

Commemorative mug, 1841

The Christening of the Prince of Wales in St George's Chapel, Windsor, 1842, by Sir George Hayter. The Duchess of Buccleuch is on the Archbishop's right.

Duke of Wellington and Sword of State and a somebody with an enormous silver mace on each side of me. Before me were numberless 'broad backs', and occasionally I could just see half the Queen's head through a crevice between elbows. When the Duchess of Buccleuch set off to do her arduous part, taking the Prince of Wales and giving him up to, and then taking him back from, the Archbishop, she made a little room, and I forced my way into it, so as to see the child perfectly, and also how well she did it, and how neatly she picked His Royal Highness, mantle and lace and all, out of the voluminous folds of the Primate's lawn sleeves and the dangers of his wig, which it was feared the Prince might have laid hold of and brought away at least on quitting his arms. I did not even see what I heard admired – the Queen's very devout and affecting manner of kneeling quite down, in spite of her cumbrous robes of the Garter, on first entering the Chapel.

Poor Archbishop Howley, whose wig had been in such peril. had not heard the last of it. Two years later, at the christening of Prince Alfred, the little Prince of Wales 'at the grand *réunion* just after the christening in the corridor, after asking two or three people and getting no answer, went up to the Archbishop himself, and said, "What is that you have got upon your head?" The Archbishop stooped down close to him, and with great respect and gentleness answered, "It is called a wig." Made a great laugh. . . .' It is perhaps not surprising that he was the last archbishop to wear a wig.

Even Victoria could not prevent occasional mishaps. Princess Alice's christening in 1843 was marred by the deliberate non-appearance of one of her godfathers, the Queen's uncle, Ernest, King of Hanover, and at Princess Louise's, in 1848, the elderly Duchess of Gloucester, forgetting where she was, suddenly got up in the middle of the service and knelt down at the Queen's feet. 'Imagine our horror!' commented Victoria.

On 16 March 1856, in the palace of the Tuileries in Paris, the Empress Eugénie presented her husband Napoleon III with a son, Napoléon-Eugène Louis Jean Joseph. Like the King of Rome before him, the baby was *ondoyé* in the palace chapel that very evening, and had a magnificent public christening at Notre-Dame three months later, on 14 June. The godparents were the Pope and the Queen of Sweden, both represented by proxies. From the palace to the cathedral, the streets were lined with crowds of people watching the dazzling procession. Everything was of the best: even the horses that drew the carriages had been specially hired from London for the occasion. Six thousand guests pressed into the cathedral, where the tiny focus of all this splendour behaved with perfect poise, looking about without a whimper and reaching out his hands. His outfit had been made by Mlle Félicie of the Rue Vivienne, who had also been responsible for the elaborate layette that the Parisians had flocked to admire before his birth. Now he appeared in a robe of Alençon needlepoint – the most costly kind of lace there was – lined with blue satin, a cap of the same, an embroidered white silk mantle, a cloak of embroidered white taffeta trimmed with lace and embroidered silk socks. He was carried on a cushion of Alençon lace and his outfit was completed by a handkerchief worked with his coat of arms. Throughout the service his father remained impassive, but when the baby was placed in his arms he suddenly came to life and held him aloft. Eugénie was so moved that she could hardly stand, and sank into a chair. This time as the imperial family emerged from the cathedral and returned to the palace, an exultant crowd cheered them all the way. Eugénie admitted later that her feelings of happiness and pride had been mingled with foreboding; justifiably so, since the child who, the Bonapartists hoped, was to establish the Napoleonic dynasty once and for all, was killed by Zulus while on a military expedition in South Africa at the age of twenty-three, his father having been deposed eight years earlier.

In 1858 Queen Victoria's daughter Vicky was herself married and about to become a mother. The detailed correspondence between the two illustrates not only how different German customs were from English ones, but what a long way Victoria had come from her royal predecessors in terms of delicacy and refinement. In October she wrote to Vicky:

> Above all promise me never to do so improper and indecorous a thing as to be lying in a dressing gown on a sofa at a christening! It would shock people here very much, and as my daughter and an English Princess I expect you will not do it. Conform to all what is reasonable, right – and essential, but in what is absurd and affected set a good example. In former times ladies received visits in their beds; Queen Charlotte also lay on a bed, at her children's christenings!! Let German ladies do what they like but the English Princess must not.

Poor Vicky, who was only eighteen and trying to steer a course between unpopularity in her new home and criticism from her old, wrote back with all the firmness and tact she could muster:

> My first duties are here now, and in fulfilling them to the utmost I can only be doing what my own country would wish and expect. . . . Therefore as to the possibility of being like the other princesses here, on a sofa at the event of a christening, I can give no promise against; ask dear Papa whether he does not think I am right. It would seem strange if a German princess married in England and insisted on having a christening there with the same customs observed as in her home. I fear I should make myself justly disliked if I showed a

contempt for a custom which is after all an innocent one – of sitting on an armchair or chaise lounge and, as the ladies do here, is natural when their children are christened at three weeks of age as they always are here. I cannot say that I see anything indecent in the custom, no more would you if you saw it, dear Mama, but from far it does sound most extraordinary. I remember last year I was horrified when I heard of Louise of Baden lying on a sofa to receive her congratulations but now that I have seen, there is really nothing indecorous in it; the Princess of Prussia sat in an armchair.

Vicky's son was born, and the christening preparations began. The German court did things on a grander scale than the English, and Vicky was clearly nervous about it, for her mother wrote to her in February 1859:

42 sponsors is somewhat alarming but never mind; I am sure you will look upon us and the Prince and Princess and Grandmama as peculiar sponsors, more really so, than most of the others. I am glad that the christening is put off till the 5th, as, backward as you are [Vicky had had a very bad time giving birth], you would have been much shaken and agitated by the pleasure and emotion of such an interesting scene. . . . Please God: the next one I shall see at its christening though I hope there won't be one for a good long time.

Queen Victoria lived to see the christenings not only of her grandchildren but of her great-grandchildren, travelling to Richmond in 1894, at the age of seventy-five, to see the future Edward VIII christened, and to be photographed with the baby, his father and his grandfather, and in 1895 presenting the future George VI with an unusual christening present in the shape of a bust of her dear departed Albert.

In the twentieth century royal christenings have been family occasions rather than State ceremonies, the public glimpsing nothing more than an official photograph released later. When the present Queen was baptized in the chapel of Buckingham Palace, on 29 May 1926, there were only six sponsors and the guests enjoyed a simple cake decorated with white York roses and a silver cradle. Prince Charles's christening, on 16 December 1948, took place in the white and gold music-room of the palace because the chapel had been damaged by German bombers in the recent war. A further sign of the times was the low sugar content of the cake, which conformed to post-war rationing. The Prince was held by his aunt, Margaret, and had seven other sponsors. His great-grandmother, Queen Mary, noted that her gift to him was 'a silver gilt cup and cover which George III had given to a godson in 1780 so that I gave a present from my great-grandfather to my great-grandson 168 years later'.

The christenings of Prince William and Prince Harry were equally private. Their parents are daily subjected to a degree of harassment from the media such as none of their predecessors had to endure. The Princess's pregnancies were announced at a very early stage and she then had to contend with months of general discussion and speculation about her state of health and even the details of her impending labour. In view of this appropriation of their private lives, one can both understand and commend the determination with which the royal couple have made sure that their children's christenings, at least, shall not be public property.

Yet despite the small scale and the privacy of these occasions, the silk and lace christening robe, the silver gilt font, the strings of names and the illustrious godparents remain unchanged, a reminder that, even in our populist times, royal babies are very special indeed.

ENVOY

These have we named; on life's rough sea they sail,
With many a prosperous, many an adverse gale!
Where passion soon, like powerful winds, will rage,
And prudence, wearied, with their strength engage.
George Crabbe, *The Parish Register*

REFERENCES

⸺◦⊙◦⸺

INTRODUCTION

The Alternative Service Book. London: Hodder & Stoughton, 1980.

The Book of Common Prayer. 1662.

George Eliot, *Silas Marner.* 1861.

Thomas Hardy, *Under the Greenwood Tree.* 1872.

Mary Corbett Harris, *Crafts, Customs and Legends of Wales.* Newton Abbot: David & Charles, 1980.

William Holland, *Paupers and Pig Killers: The Diary of William Holland a Somerset Parson 1799–1818*, ed. Jack Ayres. Gloucester: Alan Sutton, 1984.

K.S. Inglis, *Churches and the Working Classes in Victorian England.* London: Routledge & Kegan Paul, 1963.

Margaret Killip, *The Folklore of the Isle of Man.* London: Batsford, 1975.

D.H. Lawrence, *The Christening* in *The Prussian Officer.* London: Duckworth, 1914.

Martha Martin, *O Rugged Land of Gold.* New York: Macmillan, 1953.

Grandma Moses, *My Life's History.* London: André Deutsch, 1952.

The Oxford Dictionary of the Christian Church, ed. F.L. Cross and E.A. Livingstone. Oxford: Oxford University Press, 2nd ed., 1974.

Flora Thompson, *Lark Rise to Candleford.* Oxford: Oxford University Press, 1945.

Lady Clementine Waring (ed.), *Mother and Babe.* London: Putnam, 1933.

James Woodforde, *Diary of a Country Parson 1758–1781*, ed. John Beresford. Oxford: Oxford University Press, 1924.

Émile Zola, *La Terre.* 1887.

1 THE CEREMONY

St Augustine, *Confessions.* Harmondsworth, Middx: Penguin, 1961.

Georgina Battiscombe, *Charlotte Mary Yonge.* London: Constable, 1943.

H.S. Bennett, *The Pastons and Their England.* Cambridge: Cambridge University Press, 1922.

The Book of Common Prayer.

Kate Caffrey, *The Mayflower.* London: André Deutsch, 1974.

Jane Welsh Carlyle, *Letters and Memorials,* ed. J.A. Froude. London: Longmans, 1883.

L.W. Cowie, *A Dictionary of British Social History*. London: G. Bell, 1973.

Revd E.L. Cutts, *Parish Priests and Their People in the Middle Ages in England*. London: SPCK, 1914.

Dante, *The Inferno*, trans. D.L. Sayers. Harmondsworth, Middx: Penguin, 1949.

Debrett's Etiquette and Modern Manners. London: Debrett's, 1981.

Charles Dickens, *Dombey and Son*. 1847–8.

John Evelyn, *Diary*, ed. E.S. de Beer. Oxford: Oxford University Press, 1959.

Antonia Fraser, *Mary Queen of Scots*. London: Weidenfeld & Nicolson, 1969.

Abbot Gasquet, DD, *Parish Life in Medieval England*. London: Methuen, 1906.

Frances and Joseph Gies, *Life in a Medieval City*. London: Arthur Barker, 1969.

Thomas Hardy, *Tess of the d'Urbervilles*. 1891.

Dorothy Hartley, *The Land of England*. London: Macdonald, 1979.

Christina Hole, *English Home Life*. London: Batsford, 1947.

William Holland, *Paupers and Pig Killers*.

Revd Francis Kilvert, *Diary*, ed. William Plomer. London: Jonathan Cape, 3 vols, 1938–40.

Flora Klickmann (ed.), *The Etiquette of Today*. Modern Home Series, no date (*c*. 1908–10).

The Ladies Treasury. c. 1860.

D.H. Lawrence, *The Christening*.

London Society. Jan.–June 1870.

Sybil Marshall, *Fenland Chronicle*. Cambridge: Cambridge University Press, 1967.

Martha Martin, *O Rugged Land of Gold*.

Sir James Melville of Halhill, *Memoirs*, ed. Gordon Donaldson. London: Folio Society, 1969.

The Merthyr Historian, vol. 3. Merthyr Tydfil Historical and Civic Society, 1980.

Carola Oman, *An Oxford Childhood*. London: Hodder & Stoughton, 1976.

The Oxford Dictionary of the Christian Church.

Samuel Pepys, *Diary*, ed. Henry B. Wheatley. London: G. Bell, 1938.

Viscountess Ridley (ed.), *Cecilia: The Life and Letters of Cecilia Ridley 1819–1845*. London: Rupert Hart-Davis, 1958.

Douglas B.W. Sladen (ed.), *Australian Ballads and Rhymes*. London, 1888.

W.E. Tate, *The Parish Chest*. Cambridge: Cambridge University Press, 1946.

Flora Thompson, *Still Glides the Stream*. Oxford: Oxford University Press, 1948.

F.P. and M.M. Verney (eds), *Verney Memoirs*. London: Longmans Green, 1904.

James Woodforde, *Diary of a Country Parson*.

Charlotte M. Yonge, *The Daisy Chain*. London, 1856.

2 FOLKLORE

Margaret Baker, *Folklore and Customs of Rural England*. Newton Abbot: David & Charles, 1974.

Mary Clive (ed.), *From the Diary and Family Papers of Mrs Archer Clive (1801–1873)*. London: Bodley Head, 1949.

M.A. Courtney, *Cornish Feasts and Folklore*. London: Beare, 1890 (repr. EP Publishing, 1973).

L.W. Cowie, *A Dictionary of British Social History*.

Roger Fulford (ed.), *Dearest Child: Letters between Queen Victoria and the Princess Royal 1858-61*. London: Evans, 1964.

Abbot Gasquet, *Parish Life in Medieval England*.

Mary Corbett Harris, *Crafts, Customs and Legends of Wales*.

William Henderson, *Folklore of the Northern Counties of England and the Borders*. 1866 (repr. EP Publishing, 1973).

Douglas Hill, *Magic and Superstition*. London: Paul Hamlyn, 1968.

Christina Hole, *English Folklore*. London: Batsford, 1940.

A. Hamilton Jenkin, *Cornwall and the Cornish*. London: Dent, 1933.

Margaret Killip, *The Folklore of the Isle of Man*.

Maria Leach (ed.), *Standard Dictionary of Folklore, Mythology and Legend*. New York: Funk & Wagnalls, 1949.

Martha Martin, *O Rugged Land of Gold*.

Kingsley Palmer, *The Folklore of Somerset*. London, Batsford, 1976.

Enid Porter, *The Folklore of East Anglia*. London: Batsford, 1974.

Marjorie Rowling, *The Folklore of the Lake District*. London: Batsford, 1976.

Simone Sekers, *Grandmother's Lore*. London: Hodder & Stoughton, 1980.

Jacqueline Simpson, *The Folklore of the Welsh Border*. London: Batsford, 1976.

Lou Taylor, *Mourning Dress*. London: Allen & Unwin, 1983.

Flora Thompson, *Still Glides the Stream*.

Alison Uttley, *The Button-Box and Other Essays*. London: Faber & Faber, 1968.

Marcus Woodward, *The Mistress of Stantons Farm*. London: Heath Cranton, 1938.

3 NAMES

Revd B.J. Armstrong, *A Norfolk Diary*, ed. H.B.J. Armstrong. London: Harrap, 1949.

Georgina Battiscombe, *Charlotte Mary Yonge*.

Helen Cox, *Mr and Mrs Charles Dickens Entertain at Home*. Oxford: Pergamon Press, 1970.

George Crabbe, *Selections from His Poetry*, ed. Frank Whitehead. London: Chatto & Windus, 1955.

Charles Dickens, *Oliver Twist*. 1837-8.

Revd E.B. Ellnan, *Recollections of a Sussex Parson*. London, 1912.

John Evelyn, *Diary*.

Oliver Goldsmith, *The Vicar of Wakefield*. 1766.

Thomas Hardy, *Tess of the d'Urbervilles*.

William Henderson, *Folklore of the Northern Counties of England and the Borders*.

Douglas Hill, *Magic and Superstition*.

Christina Hole, *English Folklore*.

Margaret Killip, *The Folklore of the Isle of Man.*

Maria Leach (ed.), *Standard Dictionary of Folklore, Mythology and Legend.*

London Society. Jan.–June 1870.

Elizabeth Longford, *Victoria R.I.* London: Weidenfeld & Nicolson, 1964.

Antony and Peter Miall, *The Victorian Nursery Book.* London: Pantheon Books, 1980.

Sophia Morrison (ed.), *Manx Fairy Tales.* Douglas, IOM: L. Morrison, 1929 (repr. Manx Museum and National Trust, 1971).

E. Nesbit, *Five Children and It.* London: T. Fisher Unwin, 1902.

Carola Oman, *An Oxford Childhood.*

The Oxford Dictionary of English Christian Names, ed. E.G. Withycombe. Oxford: Oxford University Press, 2nd ed., 1950.

Samuel Pepys, *Diary.*

Una Pope-Hennessy, *Charles Dickens.* London: Chatto & Windus, 1945.

Enid Porter, *The Folklore of East Anglia.*

Rowland Purton, *Festivals and Celebrations.* Oxford: Basil Blackwell, 1981.

Jacqueline Simpson, *The Folklore of the Welsh Border.*

Douglas Stewart and Nancy Keesing (eds), *Australian Bush Ballads.* North Ride, NSW: Angus & Robertson, 1955.

George R. Stewart, *American Given Names.* New York: Oxford University Press, 1979.

John Stroud, *The Shorn Lamb.* London: Longmans Green, 1960.

W.E. Tate, *The Parish Chest.*

Flora Thompson, *Still Glides the Stream.*

Anthony Trollope, *Is He Popenjoy?* 1878.

Verney Memoirs.

4 GIFTS

Army & Navy Stores Catalogue 1907. (Newton Abbot: David & Charles repr., *Yesterday's Shopping,* 1969.)

Army & Navy Stores Catalogue 1898–1913. (Newton Abbot: David & Charles repr., *Edwardian Shopping,* 1975.)

L.W. Cowie, *A Dictionary of British Social History.*

Phillis Cunnington and Catherine Lucas, *Costume for Births, Marriages and Deaths.* London: A. & C. Black, 1972.

Debrett's Etiquette and Modern Manners.

Charles Dickens, *Dombey and Son.*

——, *Sketches by Boz.* 1836–7.

Alice Morse Earle, *Two Centuries of Costume in America.* New York: Macmillan, 1903 (Mineola, NY: Dover, repr. 1970).

The Enquirer's Homebook. London: Ward Lock, 1910.

Enquire Within Upon Everything. London, 1865.

John Evelyn, *Diary.*

Farmhouse Fare. Wallington, Surrey: Farmers Weekly, 1940.

G.J. Monson Fitzjohn, *Drinking Vessels of Bygone Days*. London: Herbert Jenkins, 1927.

Abbot Gasquet, *Parish Life in Medieval England*.

Sylvia Groves, *The History of Needlework Tools and Accessories*. London: Country Life Books, 1966.

Mary Hamilton, *The Silver Road*. London: Allan Wingate, 1951.

Mary Corbett Harris, *Crafts, Customs and Legends of Wales*.

Flora Klickmann, *The Etiquette of Today*.

The Ladies' Treasury.

Raoul Lemprière, *Customs, Ceremonies and Traditions of the Channel Islands*. London: Robert Hale, 1976.

Antony and Peter Miall, *The Victorian Nursery Book*.

Nicholas Harris Nicolas, *Privy Purse Expenses of Elizabeth of York/Wardrobe Accounts of Edward IV*. London: William Pickering, 1830 (repr. Frederick Muller, 1972).

Samuel Pepys, *Diary*.

Una Pope-Hennessy, *Charles Dickens*.

Miss Read, *Village Diary*. London: Michael Joseph, 1957.

Viscountess Ridley (ed.), *Cecilia*.

Marjorie Rowling, *The Folklore of the Lake District*.

Simone Sekers, *Grandmother's Lore*.

Joseph Strutt, *The Dress and Habits of the People of England*. 1842 (Tabard Facsimile repr., no date).

W.M. Thackeray, *Vanity Fair*. 1847-8.

Gladys Scott Thomson, *Life in a Noble Household 1641-1700*. London: Jonathan Cape, 1937.

Thomas Turner, *Diary*, ed. David Vaisey. Oxford: Oxford University Press, 1984.

Verney Memoirs.

James Woodforde, *Diary of a Country Parson*.

Émile Zola, *L'Assommoir*. 1877.

——, *La Terre*.

5 CLOTHES

Army & Navy Stores Catalogue 1907.

Army & Navy Stores Catalogue 1898-1913.

Stella Blum (ed.), *Victorian Fashions and Costumes from Harper's Bazaar, 1867-1898*. Mineola, NY: Dover, 1974.

Pamela Clabburn, 'My small Child bed Linning', *Costume*, 13, 1979.

Mary Clive (ed.), *From the Diary and Family Papers of Mrs Archer Clive*.

L.W. Cowie, *A Dictionary of British Social History*.

Phillis Cunnington and Anne Buck, *Children's Costume in England 1300-1900*. London: A. & C. Black, 1965.

Phillis Cunnington and Catherine Lucas, *Costume for Births, Marriages, and Deaths.*

Debrett's Etiquette and Modern Manners.

Charles Dickens, *Sketches by Boz.*

Alice Morse Earle, *Two Centuries of Costume in America.*

Enquire Within Upon Everything.

Elizabeth Gaskell, *Sylvia's Lovers.* 1863–4.

Frances and Joseph Gies, *Life in a Medieval City.*

Mary Hamilton, *The Silver Road.*

Harrod's Catalogue 1895. (Newton Abbot: David & Charles repr., *Victorian Shopping,* 1972.)

Christina Hole, *English Home Life.*

Norman Longmate, *How We Lived Then.* London: Hutchinson, 1971.

Sybil Marshall, *Fenland Chronicle.*

Martha Martin, *O Rugged Land of Gold.*

Antony and Peter Miall, *The Victorian Nursery Book.*

Barbara Morris, *Victorian Embroidery.* London: Herbert Jenkins, 1962.

Samuel Pepys, *Diary.*

Prayer Book of Edward VI. 1549.

Miss Read, *Village Diary.*

Viscountess Ridley (ed.), *Cecilia.*

W.E. Tate, *The Parish Chest.*

Flora Thompson, *Lark Rise to Candleford.*

——, *Still Glides the Stream.*

Sir Harry Verney (ed.), *The Verneys of Claydon.* Oxford: Pergamon Press, 1968.

Jane Waller (ed.), *Some Things for the Children.* London: Duckworth, 1974.

Geoffrey Warren, *A Stitch in Time: Victorian and Edwardian Needlecraft.*
Newton Abbot: David & Charles, 1976.

6 FOOD

Army & Navy Catalogue 1898–1913.

Sabine Baring-Gould, *Old Country Life.* London: Methuen, 1890.

Mrs. Beeton's Household Management. 1861.

Helen Cox, *Mr & Mrs Charles Dickens Entertain at Home.*

Debrett's Etiquette and Modern Manners.

Charles Dickens, *Dombey and Son.*

——, *Sketches by Boz.*

John Evelyn, *Diary.*

Farmhouse Fare.

Mary Hamilton, *The Silver Road.*

Harrod's Catalogue 1895.

Christina Hole, *English Home Life.*

William Jones, *Diary 1777–1821*, ed. O.F. Christie. Brentanos, 1929.

The Ladies' Treasury.

D.H. Lawrence, *The Christening.*

Raoul Lemprière, *Customs, Ceremonies and Traditions of the Channel Islands.*

Mrs Waldemar Leverton, *Little Entertainments and How to Manage Them.* London, 1904.

Martha Martin, *O Rugged Land of Gold.*

Antony and Peter Miall, *The Victorian Nursery Book.*

Peter Moss, *Meals through the Ages.* London: Harrap, 1958.

Samuel Pepys, *Diary.*

Marjorie Rowling, *The Folklore of the Lake District.*

Douglas Stewart and Nancy Keesing (eds), *Australian Bush Ballads.*

Flora Thompson, *Still Glides the Stream.*
Thomas Turner, *Diary.*
Verney Memoirs.
James Woodforde, *Diary of a Country Parson.*
Émile Zola, *L'Assommoir.*

7 ROYAL CHRISTENINGS

Octave Aubry, *Le Roi de Rome.* Paris: Arthème Fayard, 1938.
Daphne Bennett, *Queen Victoria's Children.* London: Gollancz, 1980.
Marie Louise Bruce, *Anne Boleyn.* London: Collins, 1972.
Anne Buck, *Dress in 18th Century England.* London: Batsford, 1979.
Hester Chapman, *The Last Tudor King.* London: Jonathan Cape, 1958.
Nicholas Courtney, *Royal Children.* London: Dent, 1982.
Phillis Cunnington and Catherine Lucas, *Costume for Births, Marriages and Deaths.*
David Daiches, *Charles Edward Stuart: The Life and Times of Bonnie Prince Charlie.*
    London: Thames & Hudson, 1973.
Alain Decaux, *Le Prince Impérial.* Paris: Bloud & Gay, no date.
Enquire Within Upon Everything.
Antonia Fraser, *Mary Queen of Scots.*
Roger Fulford (ed.), *Dearest Child.*
Norman Hartnell, *Royal Courts of Fashion.* London: Cassell, 1971.
John Lord Hervey, *Memoirs of the Reign of George II.* London, 1884.
Elizabeth Longford, *Victoria R.I.*
Sarah, Lady Lyttelton, *Correspondence,* ed. Mrs Hugh Wyndham. London: John
    Murray, 1912.
William of Malmesbury, *De Gestis Regum Anglorum,* ed. W. Stubbs. London:
    Rolls Series, 1887.
Sir James Melville of Halhill, *Memoirs.*
Lady Dorothy Nevill, *Life and Letters,* ed. Ralph Nevill. London: Methuen,
    1919.
Nicholas Harris Nicolas, *Privy Purse Expenses of Elizabeth of York . . .*
Elizabeth, Duchess of Northumberland, *Diaries 1716–1776,* ed. James Gray.
    London: Hodder & Stoughton, 1926.
Desmond Seward, *Prince of the Renaissance: The Life of François Ier.* London:
    Constable, 1973.
Verney Memoirs.

Appendix 1

PLANNING A CHRISTENING

No two christenings are quite the same. Although the order of service is laid down by whichever Church the child is being baptized into, the details will vary from place to place. Every priest has his own personal manner of administering the sacrament; every parish has its own customs and traditions for welcoming a new member. And when it comes to organizing the celebration afterwards, there are so few conventions to restrict you that each party can be highly individual. The notes that follow are based on my experience of my own sons' christenings, which took place in three different Church of England parishes. They are in no way definitive, but I hope they may be helpful to anyone planning a christening for the first time. Those who want further advice are recommended to consult a book such as *Debrett's Etiquette and Modern Manners.*

The ceremony and participants

It is best to begin by choosing the godparents, one of each sex for a Catholic christening, two of the child's own and one of the opposite sex for a Church of England one. Uncles and aunts are a common choice, but any relative or long-standing friend can be enlisted. Most people are delighted and flattered to be asked, but if for some reason they should be reluctant to accept, it would be wrong to press them. The relationship is intended to be a happy and lasting one, and it will not be if it is forced at the outset.

Once you have secured the godparents, the next step is to contact the clergyman you would like to officiate. Normally this will be your own parish priest, but if you have a friend or relation in orders whom you wish to ask to conduct the service in your local church, you must of course obtain the resident priest's approval. You can approach the clergyman in person, by letter or by telephone, but he will certainly want to arrange a meeting, as there will be many details to discuss. First, and especially if you are not already known to him, he will want to have some idea of your own religious background and commitment, and if you are not a practising Christian he may suggest that a service of thanksgiving would be more appropriate than a baptism. This depends very much on the views of the individual priest. If you decide on a baptism, the Church of England offers two possible orders of service. Most churches nowadays have adopted the rite provided in *The Alternative Service Book* of 1980, which uses simple language, stresses the concept of community fellowship, and involves the entire congregation in the responses. But if you wish, you may follow instead *The Book of Common Prayer* of 1662. The language here is old-fashioned and much more poetic, and the doctrine of original sin is emphasized, which many people find unacceptable. We chose this rite for our eldest son's christening because we liked the poetry and embraced the theology, but the rector expressed some surprise at our choice. Whichever form you opt for, the ceremony will be integrated into the usual Sunday service. In the Catholic Church there is only one rite, and here it is not uncommon to hold a christening on its own, and not always on a Sunday.

The priest will next inquire into the religious background of the godparents, and will want to be sure that they, as well as you, are aware of what they are undertaking. In theory they should be baptized and confirmed members of the appropriate Church, but in practice members of other Christian Churches are acceptable. Thus our eldest son's godparents were composed of a Catholic, a Methodist and a Pentecostal. If, however, your chosen godparents are not even nominal Christians, the priest may suggest that you reconsider your choice.

There are practical details to be thought out too. You may be asked how large a party you anticipate bringing to church, so that pews may be reserved for you. You might want to request a particular hymn. For our eldest son's christening we were able to choose one of the hymns from our wedding, and for that of the youngest his elder brothers chose their own favourite. When all these matters have been sorted out, you can arrange a mutually convenient date for the ceremony. In many parishes it is customary to baptize several children on the same occasion. Our second son shared his christening with a baby from a few doors away.

Parents and godparents are often nervous before the ceremony, but there is no need to be. The priest will give them very clear instructions when he wants them to proceed to the font, put their hands on the child or make responses. In any case, it is important to remember that this is a joyful occasion in which the whole congregation is sharing. In the Catholic ceremony the mother holds the baby throughout; in the Church of England the godmother takes it from her at the font, and in some cases the godfather has a turn as well. It is common in many churches for all children, whether part of the christening group or not, to be invited up to the font, so that they can see what is going on. After baptism the child is generally given a lighted candle, which is intended to be preserved, but some churches dispense with this. Our first and second sons each received a card of welcome made by the Sunday school, and a charming custom at our present church is for the Mothers' Union to present the baby's mother with a posy of flowers at the end of the service.

Clothes

It is usual to dress the baby in white and, unless the family is lucky enough to have an heirloom robe, suitable outfits can be either bought or made. Instructions for reproducing a Victorian-type dress are given in Appendix 2. Bear in mind that most churches are chilly even in summer: the baby will need a warm vest and tights under its dress and some kind of pretty wrap or shawl over it. Family and guests generally wear Sunday-best clothes. The men certainly wear suits, but there is no need for the women to wear hats. If you are planning a very formal occasion and want your guests to dress up accordingly it would be wise to warn them beforehand.

Christening parties

The time of day of the service will dictate whether you have a lunch- or tea-party afterwards. The officiating priest should be invited as a matter of course, though many clergymen have so many commitments, especially on a Sunday, that they are unable to accept. Christening parties are generally small, consisting of family, close friends and perhaps neighbours. If you have spent the better part of the morning in church, you do not want a large-scale catering job on your hands as well. But if you would like to extend the celebration in some way, there are solutions that will not involve you in too much extra work. In France sugared almonds are distributed to all and sundry at the end of the ceremony. In the parish where our eldest son was baptized, and with which we were actively involved, it was the custom for the congregation to gather together for coffee at the back of the church when the service was over. On the Sunday of the christening we took along a large fruit cake baked by a grandmother, and this was cut up and given out with the coffee to everybody present. A very much smaller and more manageable party of fifteen or so then met for lunch at home.

Food is entirely a matter of personal choice, but most people find that a cold buffet is the easiest to prepare and serve. Pâtés, flans and puddings can all be prepared in advance, and there are generally plenty of willing helpers. No christening party would be complete without a cake. If you do not wish to make it yourself there are many bakers who will oblige, and who will ice it to your specifications. The child's name or initials are usually featured, and the decorations are traditionally pale blue or pink according to the baby's sex.

Presents

It is usual for all the guests to bring a present for the baby, unless the parents have specifically asked them not to. A godparent's gift is intended to be kept for life. Traditionally it is made of silver, and spoons, egg-cups or bracelets, perhaps engraved with the child's name, can be supplied by most jewellers; but this is not a fixed rule and many other ideas will be found in Chapter 4. The other guests' presents can be of a more ephemeral nature, and almost anything in the way of books, toys or nursery-ware is acceptable.

When the christening is over a note of thanks should be sent to the priest.

HOW NOT TO PLAN A CHRISTENING (1812)

In the midst of Hazlitt's weaknesses, his parental affections were beautiful. He had one boy. He loved him. He doated on him. He told me one night this boy was to be christened. 'Will ye come on Friday?' 'Certainly,' said I. His eye glistened. Friday came, but as I knew all parties I lunched heartily first and was there punctually at four. Hazlitt then lived in Milton's house, Westminster. . . . At four I came but he was out. I walked up and found his wife ill by the fire in a bed gown – nothing ready for guests, and everything wearing the appearance of neglect and indifference. I said, 'Where is Hazlitt?' 'Oh dear, William has gone to look for a parson.' 'A parson; why, has he not thought of that before?' 'No, he didn't.' 'I'll go and look for him,' said I, and out I went into the Park through Queen's Square and met Hazlitt in a rage coming home. 'Have ye got a parson?' 'No, sir,' said he, 'these fellows are all out.' 'What will ye do?' 'Nothing.' So in we walked, Hazlitt growling at all the parsons and the church.

When we came in we sat down – nobody was come; – no table laid, – no appearance of dinner. . . . I sat down, the company began to drop in – Charles Lamb and his poor sister – all sorts of odd, clever people. Still no dinner. At last came in a maid who laid a cloth and put down knives and forks in a heap. Then followed a dish of potatoes, cold, waxy and yellow. Then came a great bit of beef with a bone like a battering ram toppling on all its corners. Neither Hazlitt nor Lamb seemed at all disturbed, but set to work helping each other! while the boy, half clean and obstinate, kept squalling to put his fingers into the gravy.
From Benjamin Haydon's *Autobiography and Journals*, ed. Tom Taylor, 1853.

Appendix 2

HOW TO MAKE A VICTORIAN CHRISTENING ROBE

The guidelines for making a christening robe given on pages 86/88 are too vague to be of much use to the present-day dressmaker. The measurements (when they are specified at all) are unreliable, and many points of construction are omitted altogether, no doubt on the assumption that they are too obvious to need describing. The instructions below have been adapted for the purpose of producing a similar but slightly less elaborate robe copied from a late Victorian one in the author's possession. (See sketch and diagrams pp. 152, 153.)

You will need

1.5 metres of plain white cotton fabric 90 cm wide, e.g. lawn or voile. A firm weave is best if you are to make the pin-tucks successfully. You are not recommended to use polyester cotton or any other synthetic fabric: the feel and hang will not be right and the easy-care properties will be wasted on a dress designed to be worn a few times at most.
3.25 metres of white cotton embroidered insertion 2.5 cm wide.
3.25 metres of white cotton embroidered edging 5 cm wide.
3.75 metres of white cotton embroidered edging 10 cm wide.
0.75 metre of white lace 1 cm wide.
1.5 metres of white ribbon 0.5 cm wide.

To make the tucked fabric

The centre front (CF) panels of both bodice and skirt consist of alternating horizontal bands of insertion and tucked cotton fabric. Start by making up the tucks. Cut three strips, each 10 cm wide, across the whole width of your fabric. Take the first strip and fold it parallel to, and 3 cm from, one long edge. Stitch 4 mm from fold. Fold again, 15 mm from line of stitching, and again stitch 4 mm from fold. Repeat once more. You should now have a strip 90 cm long and 7.5 cm wide, with three parallel tucks along it. Now make tucks in the other two strips in the same way.

To make the CF panels

To make the CF skirt panel take a piece of strong paper and cut out a wedge shape, 8.5 cm wide at the top, 38 cm at the bottom, and 67.5 cm long. Mark it out in pencil according to diagram 1. A 2.5 cm strip of insertion runs right down the middle, and the sides are divided into horizontal bands, alternately 7.5 cm and 2.5 cm wide. When you have marked out the paper, cut your strips of insertion and tucked fabric to fit, *not forgetting* to add 6 mm to all the short edges to allow for the seams. (The seam allowance is already provided for on the long edges of the tucked fabric.) Now sew all the strips together, making up the two sides first and then joining them to the vertical central strip. The best way to do this is to lay the insertion flat over the raw edges of the tucked fabric and sew it down either with a fine machine stitch or with small running stitches. Keep checking against the paper pattern that the size and shape stay correct. Now make the bodice panel in exactly the same way, scaling up diagram 2 to get the right shape. Note that the full width of the tucked fabric is not needed, so you must centre the pin-tucks accurately on each of the four horizontal bands and trim away the surplus fabric from the seam allowances.

To complete the skirt

Cut two pieces of the 5 cm edging, each 1 metre long. Gather them both up to 69.5 cm. With right sides together tack one piece of edging to each side of the CF skirt panel. Now cut a piece of the cotton fabric measuring 120 cm by 67.5 cm. Cut it in half across the width and, with a narrow French seam, sew it up again to within 10 cm of what is now the top edge. Neaten the opening, which is now the centre back. Now shape the short sides of your piece of fabric to fit the CF panel. Mark a point on the bottom edge 14.5 cm in from the corner. Draw a straight line from this point to the top corner and cut away the resulting triangle. Now join the edges you have just shaped to the sides of the CF panel with a French seam, enclosing the embroidered frill. Cut off 3.25 metres of the 10 cm edging, gather it up to fit the bottom of the skirt and stitch it in place, enclosing the end of the vertical frill at each side.

To make the bodice and sleeves

Scale up diagrams 3, 4 and 5. Cut the bodice backs and side fronts from the cotton fabric and the sleeves from the remainder of the 10 cm embroidery: its scalloped edging will form a decorative finish. Allow 6 mm extra for seams on all the raw edges. Mark off the centre 6 cm of the sleeve-head and gather up to 5 cm. Using a very narrow French seam, join the underarm seams of both bodice and sleeves, and stitch the ungathered parts of the sleeve-head to the bodice armholes at back and front. The gathered portion thus forms part of the neckline. Form the tucks in the bodice backs, tack them in place at the top and bottom, and press them towards the centre back. Neaten the centre back edges. Now cut the remainder of the 5 cm edging in half. Each of these pieces is going to go up one side of the CF panel, over the shoulder and along the back neck edge. Gather them up to fit. Join the side fronts of the bodice to the CF panel, right sides together, enclosing the frill. Tack the remainder of the frill to the sleeve-head and the back neck edge. From the remaining cotton fabric cut 2 or 3 bias strips 3 cm wide and join them until you have enough length to fit round the neck edge. Bind the raw edge. Gather up the lace to fit and attach it to the neck edge, stitching it to the seam you have just made so that it stands up and covers the binding. Neaten the whole of the lower edge of the bodice with a tiny hem.

To finish

The waistband is a straight strip of insertion 56 cm long. Gather up the top edge of the skirt to fit it and join them together by laying the insertion flat over the line of gathering and stitching it down. Fold the insertion in half and catch the free edge down on the wrong side, enclosing the gathers. Now stitch the folded edge down on to the lower edge of the bodice, making your seam as close to the fold as possible. Cut the ribbon in half and slot it through the channels formed by the waistband and the neck binding.

This robe should fit a baby up to the age of about ten months. It can be made larger by increasing the waistband and letting out the bodice tucks.

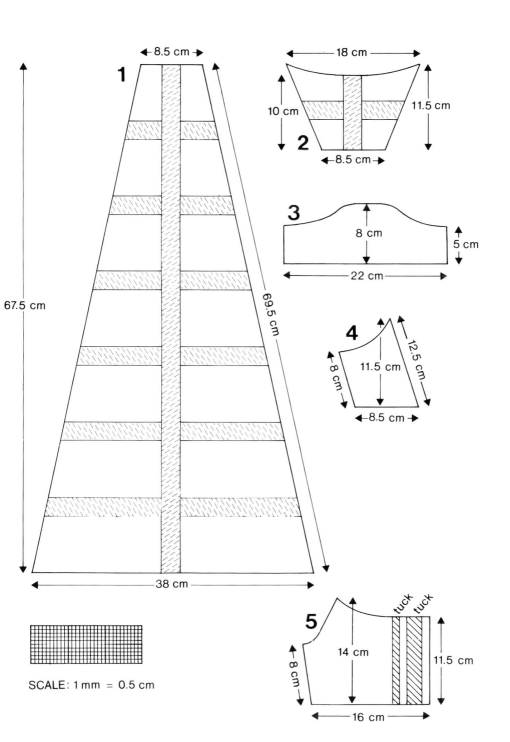

1

← 8.5 cm →

67.5 cm

69.5 cm

38 cm

2

18 cm

10 cm

11.5 cm

← 8.5 cm →

3

8 cm

5 cm

22 cm

4

12.5 cm

8 cm

11.5 cm

← 8.5 cm →

5

tuck   tuck

14 cm

8 cm

11.5 cm

16 cm

SCALE: 1 mm = 0.5 cm

Appendix 3

RECIPES

The recipes that follow have been included chiefly for historical interest rather than with a view to their being reproduced in the modern kitchen. Ingredients, cooking methods and tastes have all changed, all of which should be borne in mind if disappointments are to be avoided. Nevertheless it is interesting to see what Parson Woodforde would have meant by a 'blamange', and how the tarts and custards enjoyed by Thomas Turner differed from ours. The majority of the recipes are taken from seventeenth- and eighteenth-century cookery books. Recipes 1, 2, 6 and 7 are taken from *Meals through the Ages* by Peter Moss (Harrap, 1958), and recipes 4, 13 and 15 come from *Farmhouse Fare*, a collection of traditional country recipes first published in 1940 by *Farmers Weekly*.

1 ROASTED PIG
Spit your Pig and lay it to the Fire, which must be a very good one. Before you lay it down, take a little Sage, a piece of butter as big as a Walnut, and a little Pepper and Salt. Put them into the Pig and sew it up with a coarse thread, and flour it all over very well and keep flouring till the Eyes drop out. Be sure to save all the Gravy that come out of it. When the Pig is done enough stir the fire up brisk; take a coarse cloth, with about a quarter of a pound of Butter in it, and rub the Pig all over till the Crackling is quite crisp, then take it up. Melt some good butter, boil it with the gravy you saved and pour it into the Dish with the Brains and the Sage all mixed together, and send it to the table.
Hannah Glasse, *The Art of Cookery made Plain and Easy*, 1748.

2 A RAISED DUCKLING PYE

Take the livers of your ducklings and make a little forcemeat with a little scraped bacon, a mushroom or two, some herbs, pepper, salt, and nutmeg, pounded well together, a morsel of soft bread and an egg or two; mix it well and put it into the ducklings. Put them into your crust with a bunch of onions and parsley, cover them with slices of bacon and finish your making. Before you send it to table take a little broth and cullis [meat jelly] mixt; take out your bacon and fat, and pour in your sauce with the juice of a lemon and serve up without the lid.
William Verral, *Complete System of Cookery*, 1759.

3 TO BAKE A SWAN

Scald it, and take out the bones: then parboyle it and season it well with pepper, salt and ginger. Then lard it, and put it in a deepe coffin [i.e. pastry case] of rye paste, with store of butter. Let it soake well. When you take it out of the oven put in more butter moulten at the vent-hole.
Jane Mosley's *Derbyshire Recipes*, 1669–1712 (Derbyshire Museum Service, 1979).

N.B. It is not advisable to try out this recipe today, as swans are Crown property. Their consumption is restricted to members of St John's College, Cambridge, at the supper of their annual May Ball. The privilege has not been exercised since 1926, however, except in a symbolic way: a wax effigy of a swan's neck is affixed to a humbler bird, such as a turkey, and it is on this that the members now feast.

4 FOWL PUDDING WITH MUSHROOMS

2 chickens cut up in joints; a few slices of fat bacon; 4 large sage leaves chopped fine; tablespoonful chopped onion; pepper and salt to taste; $\frac{1}{4}$lb suet; $\frac{1}{2}$lb flour; good plate of mushrooms.
Line a good-sized pudding basin with a suet crust, put in a layer of chicken, chopped sage and onion, then a layer of peeled mushrooms, and continue until the basin is filled. Sprinkle plenty of flour between each layer, as that makes good thick gravy. The slices of bacon should be cut up in thin strips and put in each layer. Nearly fill the basin with

water, cover with suet crust, and steam for about 3 hours. This is a very tasty and nourishing dish.
Farmhouse Fare.

The original recipe uses rabbits, the substitution of chickens being the present writer's. The switch seemed justifiable in view of the close similarity between this recipe and Marianna's pudding.

5 To Make a Plain Pudding

Weigh three-quarters of a pound of any odd scraps of bread, whether crust or crumb, cut them small, and pour on them a pint and a half of boiling water, to soak them well. Let it stand till the water is cool, then press it out, and mash the bread smooth with the back of a spoon. Add to it, a tea-spoonful of beaten ginger, some moist sugar, and three-quarters of a pound of currants. Mix all well together, and lay it in a pan well buttered. Flatten it down with a spoon, and lay some pieces of butter on the top. Bake it in a moderate oven, and serve it hot. When cold, it will turn out of the pan, and eat like good plain cheese cakes.
English 18th Century Cookery (Roy Bloom, no date).

6 To Make Rice Pudding

Take a quarter of a pound of rice and put it into a saucepan with a quart of new milk, a stick of cinnamon. Stir it often to keep it from sticking to the saucepan. When it is boiled thick pour it into a pan; stir in a quarter of a pound of fresh butter and sugar to your taste. Grate half a nutmeg, add three or four spoonfuls of rosewater and stir all together. When it is cold beat up eight eggs and four whites and beat it all together. Butter a dish and pour it all in and bake it.
Hannah Glasse, op. cit.

7 To Make an Apple Pye

Make a good puff-paste Crust, lay some round the Sides of the dish, pare and quarter your Apples, and take out the cores; lay a Row of Apples thick, throw in half your sugar, mince a little Lemon-peel, throw

over and squeeze a little lemon over them and the rest of the sugar . . .
boil the Pelings of the Apples, and Cores, in some water with a Blade of
mace till it is very good; pour it into your pye, put on your Upper crust
and bake it. When they come out of the oven, you may beat up the yolks
of two Eggs and half a pint of Cream, with a little Nutmeg sweetened
with Sugar, take off the Lid and pour in the Cream.
Ibid.

8 Baked Custards
Boil a pint of cream with some mace and cinnamon, and when it is cold,
take four yolks of eggs, a little rose water, sack, nutmeg, and sugar, to
taste; mix them well and bake them.
English 18th Century Cookery.

9 Almond Custards
Blanch a quarter of a pound of almonds, beat them very fine, and then
put them into a pint of cream, with two spoonsful of rose water; sweeten
it, and put in the yolks of four eggs; stir them well together till it becomes
thick, and then pour it into cups.
Ibid.

10 To Make Blancmange
Put into 1 quart of water an ounce of isinglass, and let it boil till it is
reduced to a pint, then put in the whites of 4 eggs with 2 spoonsful of rice
water, and sweeten it to taste. Run it through a jelly bag, and then put to
it 2 ounces of sweet, and 1 ounce of bitter almonds. Scald them in the
jelly, and then run them through a hair sieve. Put it into a China bowl
and the next day turn it out. Garnish with flowers or green leaves, and
stick all over the top blanched almonds cut lengthways.
Ibid.

11 To Make Paste for Tarts
Put an ounce of loaf sugar, beat and sifted, to one pound of fine flour.

Make it into a stiff paste, with a gill of boiling cream, and three ounces of butter. Work it well, and roll it very thin.
Ibid.

12 To Make Almond Tarts

Blanch and beat some fine almonds, with a little white wine and some sugar (a pound of sugar to a pound of almonds), grated bread, nutmeg, cream, and the juice of spinach, to colour the almonds. Bake it in a gentle oven, and when done, thicken with candied orange peel or citron.
Ibid.

13 Damson Cheese

Put some sound ripe fruit into a stone jar (or casserole), cover it, and bake in a very cool oven until the damsons are tender. Then drain off the juice, skin and stone the fruit, and put it into a preserving-pan. Pour back on them from a third, to half, of their juice, and boil over a clear fire until they form a dry paste. Add fine sugar, in the proportion of 6ozs. to each pound of the fruit. Then stir continuously over the fire until the sugar has dissolved, and the fruit comes away dry from the sides of the pan. Press it into small jars, or moulds, and when perfectly cold place on the top of each a round of paper that has been dipped in spirit. Fasten securely, and store in a dry place. Will keep for months.
Farmhouse Fare.

14 Bride or Christening Cake

Ingredients: $3\frac{1}{2}$lbs. of the finest flour, 3lbs. of fresh butter, $7\frac{1}{2}$lbs. of currants, 3lbs. of raw sugar, 2 grated nutmegs, $\frac{1}{4}$ of an oz. of mace, $\frac{3}{4}$ of an oz. of cloves, 24 eggs, 1lb. of sweet whole blanched almonds, $\frac{1}{2}$ a lb. of candied citron, $\frac{3}{4}$ of a lb. each of candied orange- and lemon-peel, I gill of wine, 1 gill of brandy.

Method: Take some good strong household flour and rub it through a fine sieve on to a sheet of paper. Well wash, dry and pick the currants free from stones and sprigs, and lay them on the table ready for use. Blanch the almonds, shred the peel very fine, and mix it with the currants. Break the eggs, taking especial care to eliminate any that are bad or musty, and put them into a clean basin. Weigh the sugar and roll it on the table with a rolling-pin to break up all lumps; put it in a large pan, add the butter and all the spices in fine powder, and proceed to beat the mixture up to a light cream with the hand; add the eggs 2 at a time, allowing an interval of at least 5 minutes between each addition of eggs, beating as hard as possible all the time. When all the eggs have been put in, mix in the fruit and peel, and last of all add the flour, with the wine and spirits. When thoroughly well mixed, put it out into well papered hoops and press it down in the centre with the back of the hand, set it into a cool oven and bake for about 6 hours. This recipe will make about 24lbs. of cake, but if a fairly large oven is not available, it would be better not to bake the whole of this quantity in one hoop, or it will not make a very satisfactory cake, as the top and sides will be burnt and dried before the cake can be properly cooked. It would therefore be preferable to divide it into 2 or more smaller cakes. . . . As these cakes are better for keeping, it is advisable to make and bake them at least 3 months before they are required. If this is done, the best way to keep them is to strip off all the paper they were baked in, and then to wrap up each cake in a large sheet of rice parchment or wax paper, then wrap it up in several thicknesses of clean newspaper, pack away in a tin or airtight box, and stow away in a dry cool place. . . .

Time – To bake, 5 to 6 hours. Average Cost, 2s. per pound.
Mrs. Beeton's Household Management, 1861.

15 COVENTRY GODCAKES

12 ozs plain flour; 12 ozs margarine; pinch of salt; water to mix; mincemeat; 1 white of egg; castor sugar.

Add a pinch of salt to the flour and sieve into a basin, pour in cold water gradually and mix it to a stiff paste. It should be neither sticky nor dry, just pliable. Turn on to a floured board and knead lightly until smooth. Roll out to an oblong shape. Press out the margarine until not quite half the size of the pastry, put on the one half and fold over the other.

Press edges well together, roll out to same thickness as before, fold into three; do this twice more, but the last time roll out to about $\frac{1}{8}''$ thick. Cut out three-cornered pieces of pastry and place mincemeat in centre, place another piece of pastry on top, press well together, and make one or two cuts on top and bake in a very hot oven for about 15 minutes.

When cooked, glaze the tops with the white of egg beaten to a froth and dust castor sugar over. Return to oven for 3 minutes. Place on a sieve until cold.

Farmhouse Fare.

16 NEGUS

Ingredients – To every pint of port wine allow 1 quart of boiling water, $\frac{1}{4}$lb. of sugar, 1 lemon, grated nutmeg to taste.

Mode – The wine need not be very old or expensive for this purpose, a new fruity wine answering very well for it. Put the wine into a jug, rub some lumps of sugar (equal to a quarter of a pound) on the lemon-rind until all the yellow part of the skin is absorbed, then squeeze the juice, and strain it. Add the sugar and lemon-juice to the port, with the grated nutmeg; pour over it the boiling water, cover the jug, and, when the beverage has cooled a little, it will be fit for use. Negus may also be made of sherry, or any other sweet white wine, but is more usually made of port than of any other beverage.

Sufficient – Allow 1 pint of wine, with the other ingredients in proportion, for a party of 9 or 10 persons.

Mrs. Beeton's Household Management.

INDEX

Pages with illustrations are in italic.

163